African Urban Echoes

Published in 2025 by

Griots Lounge Publishing Canada
www.griotslounge.ca
Email: info@griotslounge.ca

African Urban Echoes: A Poetry Anthology
Poetry/Anthology

Library and Archives Canada Cataloguing in Publication

ISBN: 978-17386993-9-1

Cover and Interior Design by Sarah Peters
Cover Image by Temitope Ojo

Printed and bound in Canada.

Praise for *African Urban Echoes*

A delicious offering on the poetic imagination of African cities. In this anthology, the African city is a labyrinth of processual images and poetic sounds, weaving tapestries of human and extra-human vitalities and sensorium. The volume arrives at the right time to refresh the discourse and cadence of the urban turn in African studies. We must salute Jide Salawu and Rasaq Malik for their thoughtful calibration of urban poetics and the affordance of seeing the African city anew.

—Cajetan Iheka, Yale University

African Urban Echoes is a triumph. Across more than a hundred individual works by dozens of poets, the volume highlights the long history of African urban experiences; the global reach of migration; and the singular constancy of change. These works recall poetry's power to reflect the world and, in so doing, demand better worlds. Together, the volume highlights the tensions that characterize so much of urban life: between continuity and change; connection and alienation; and the ever-present mixtures of fear and joy. The poems in *African Urban Echoes* call to their readers with the urgency and intimacy of city streets. The collection, a worthy addition to the recent flourishing of poetry anthologies from and about Africa, will be of immense value to poetry students and enthusiasts alike.

—Susanna Sacks, Howard University

From Cairo to Cape Town the poems collected here celebrate and articulate the nuanced dynamism and incredible variances of cities across the African continent with particular attention to a new crop of contemporary poets. What's evident in this gathering of poems is the divergent interplay between aesthetics, histories, cultural traditions, migrations, and their embodiment of spaces that help shape the contours of contemporary African life. These poems are a testament to an evolution of place, both physical and imaginary, that articulate the subtlety and power of the often intangible concept of home.

—Matthew Shenoda, Brown University

African Urban Echoes is a righteous journey through the city with its poets. It is a walk filled with delight and frustration and goodness and apt observation of corners of the African continent sometimes adored and sometimes despised. You as a reader are witness to the tiny revelations of others as they shell the peas of places they call home, uncovering a story under the story and a secret under the secret . These places are changing or not, deeply historied or as new as children. For a moment, at the insistence of these poets you borrow their eyes and fingers and you become as part of their cities as they are. You are taking in Braam's breath with Zada Hanmer in Joburg, longing for Cairo with Dina El Dessouky, or walking through the Lagos rain open palms extended to catch water with Yeku James. Wherever this anthology takes you, however political or intimate or intimately political, you feel fortunate to have been invited along. This book is a triumph in curation and care for African cities.

—Upile Chisala, Malawian Poet

African Urban Echoes reverberates with the insights of poets responsive to cityscapes from Carthage to Cape Town, Accra to Kampala. The continent's megacities—Cairo, Lagos, Johannesburg—resound here. So do the "clanging pans" of New Year celebrations in Gulu and songs heard near the centuries-old city walls of Kano. "A city endures where a people endure," declares Obari Gomba. "Even in death, / your people wander," intones Patricia Jabbeh Wesley. These poems revere placemaking while recognizing that people are restless beings. Proving poets to be keen interpreters of urban lifeworlds, this anthology rightly underscores African poets' right to the city.

—Nathan Suhr-Sytsma, author of *Poetry, Print, and the Making of Postcolonial Literature*, Emory University.

AFRICAN URBAN ECHOES

A POETRY ANTHOLOGY

EDITED BY JIDE SALAWU & RASAQ MALIK

For more than two decades, poetry anthologies in African literature have navigated the shared world of African identity or living in the continent of Africa without capturing comprehensively the lifeworld of African cities. *African Urban Echoes* is a gathering of poets that seek to contribute to the echoes of resistance, hope, and anxieties all produced simultaneously by African urban centers in their polyvalences and unique characters. Poets from different African countries evoke detailed portraits of lives as cities and cities as lives. They compel us to see both the defined and undefined beauties of African cities through sublime experiences captured in disparate forms and network of images in this anthology. They immerse their readers in marginal realities of urban citizenship and turn them to witnesses of both familiar and unfamiliar landscapes from Lagos, Lome, Johannesburg to Tunis, and of places that are inevitably part of their stories as pilgrims, as travelers settling and leaving.

Contributors

Chinụa Ezenwa-Ọhaeto
Emelda Gwitimah
Fatma Latif
Tanure Ojaide
Zama Madinana
Osagiede Best
Sodiq Alabi
Rahma Jimoh
Hussain Ahmed
Salimah Valiani
S. Su'eddie Vershima Agema
Sarpong Osei Asamoah
Ojo Olumide Emmanuel
Tope Larayetan
Ridwan Badamasi
Joseph Hope
Jide Badmus
Uchechukwu Umezurike
Jumoke Verissimo
Patricia Jabbeh Wesley
Dina El Dessouky
Obari Gomba
Zada Hanmer
Ipadeola Tade
Omodero David Oghenekaro
Emmanuel Anzaku
Alma Simba
Brindley Fortuin
James Yeku
Gbemisola Adeoti
M.L. Kejera
Pamilerin Jacob
Dami Ajayi
Kordjo Senyo Amenyanoo
Nurain O. Ali-Balogun
Abdullah Olajuwon Adedokun
Okwudili Nebeolisa
Tolu Oloruntoba
Abdulrosheed Oladipupo Fasasi
Temiloluwa Okanmiyo Oluyemi
Afua Ansong
Servio Gbadamosi
Kola Tubosun
Ber Anena
Jide Salawu
Rasaq Malik Gbolahan

Contents

Preface

The interminable echoes of African cities have always been in the chambers of modern African poetry; the malleable character of the cities as avowed by AbdouMaliq Simone, Achille Mbembe, Akin Mabogunje, and many others has been a central concern of poets in the last few decades. African poetry, with its expansive lyric power, affirms this assessment as well. African poetry has always been an active data bank that acknowledges African histories, as well as the spaces, towns, and provinces of the human and more than human, with their untamable energies. The African griots in their chants, panegyrics, songs, and ballads evoke places. They celebrate empires, subjects, rulers and record the vast spaces and constituencies of power, allures of development, commerce, and arts with great resonance and examples that include Timbuktu, Bornu, Songhai, Benin, Oyo kingdom – these place names remain an allusive force in the Isidore Okpewho-edited volume, *The Heritage of African Poetry*, published by Longman in 1985. Even with the invasion of colonial masters, planners, partitioners, and scramblers, African cities have found ways of reinventing themselves. Formatted through colonial narratives and engineered neoliberal ideology in postcolonial times, the African poets transgress and rebuke the permanent personalities often allocated to their cities. These poets register a matrix of trajectories: speculative, social, economic, political, psychical and many others. And we, readers, can follow that suit our enterprise in the dynamics of their subjects.

Again, we do not attempt to claim that African urbanities have no footprint across multiplexes of poetry collections that have been assembled across generations of African writers. Far from it, we foreground in this volume that African poetic historiography has often been a repository of metropolitan knowledge, city life, and cosmopolitan experiences often injected into the speakers' minds. These personas make their intentions known in stanzas, meters, and diverse poetic forms. Specifically, modern African poetry has always had a place of gathering, and by gathering, we mean the anthology is a kind of poetry archive form and database that provides diverse perspectives, illustrations, and enchantments. African poetry as an archive irreducibly addresses African experiences. From *West African Verse: An Anthology* edited by Donatus Ibe Nwoga to *An Anthology of East African Poetry* edited by A. D. Amateshe, the poems contain footprints of African urban spirits. As editors, we were pressed by a concern that city in poem and poem in city has always appeared in fragments. There is a conspicuous absence of a sustained effort to comprehensively collect poems that bear witness to African cities. This present anthology fulfills this gap in its mission to enter poetry into the dialogue of African urbanity. As anthologizers of the poems in *African Urban Echoes*, our aim is to make a case for African urbanities and cities, encoded in their modernities and everyday rhythms.

Still, the credit belongs to the contributors who have documented and re-verbed the African urban soul through their works. They bring ultimate newness to understanding Africa through their memories, resistance of their voices, and immediacy of their tone for radical hope. While contemplating the tenacious path of the current work, we are arrested in our rumination by the short indelible image of "Ibadan" that John Pepper Clark evokes for us in the lines: "running splash of rust and gold". The image invokes a scenario in which the archeological trowel may be useful to dig further into the history of the city, its newness and datedness, its conflation of technology. The persona invites readers to witness the past and the old while reinforcing the golden present. We must not too quickly forget how Clark centers the ecology of the city with its hills. This ecology also is a way of knowing the myth of the city and its megafauna. Clark's attention is also on the ontology of the city. It refuses colonial pre-emption about African cities and their origins. This poetic brief appears in Nwoga's volume of *West African Verse* published by Longman in 1967. The anthology has remained a classic archive of modern African poetry, and Clark's "Ibadan," a solid urban stamp among the diverse themes highlighted in the volume.

Then there is the lamentation of Lennard Okola in "Their City" published as part of the generative works in *An Anthology of East African Poetry* edited by A. D. Amateshe. This anthology was originally published in 1988 by Longman. Okola implicates the East African city as a space where there is sun, but "without any warmth/except for wanaotosheka,*"—the Swahili word for the privileged. The city is, in Okola's evocation, a strait dominated and enjoyed by a social class. This is a materialist rendering of an unnamed East African city by Okola. It does not mean that many underprivileged people do not exist in this city, yet what seems to be intoned in Okola's work that is also contained in the spirit of the anthology is that urbanity has become a space of class performance. It is an uneven zone where you can find "the thickset directors of many companies." The African poet has not claimed the label of utopia for the African city. In fact, some African poets are more interested in the heterotopic characteristics of urban sprawl. Their genuine concern with its political economy is that the African city accommodates and provides hope for the masses, rather than a city hijacked by the powerful.

In 1988, Longman African Series also published *A Selection of African Poetry* edited by Kojo E. Senanu and Theo Vincent. The volume is one of the most trenchant documentations of African poetry enriched with the histories, forms, styles, tones, and powerful languages, by which modern African poetry established its pedigree. Thinking about Sensanu and Vincent's edited anthology now, our minds wander to Oswald Mtshali's poem, "Nightfall in Soweto," evoking the fear, distrust, and traumatizing noir experience of an Apartheid South African city. Mtshali's terrifying escalation of what night means in the South African neighborhood of Soweto is tellingly captured as follows: "Nightfall comes like/a dreaded disease/seeping through the pores/of a healthy body/and ravaging it beyond repair". The macabre turn of this city and urban environment registers the general political atmosphere for South Africans, who were abused and repressed under colonial rule. The city under the hegemonies of Apartheid rulers is therefore an uninhabitable zone, a necropolis, to use the effectual term of Achille Mbembe where the speaker describes themselves as a "prey" (Mtshali "Nightfall in Soweto"). In fact, night is contagious and comparing it to a disease, to be emphatic, is to signify the level of stress and the insidious damage on the body to project precarious condition and vulnerability of being Black in South Africa. Mtshali fits time and space together in order to underpin colonial brutality. Like Okola and Dennis Brutus's "Nightsong: City," there is less romanticization of the African city in this poem, unlike what Clark encourages us to look at in "Ibadan."

We believe Soyinka's edited anthology, *Poems from Black Africa*, is a definitive signifier in modern African poetry. The volume is a fistful of many thematic streams. Building the catalog of trends in African poetry is helpful for many readers and poetry enthusiasts, from Alien Perspectives, Ancestors and Gods, Animistic Phases, Black Thoughts, Captivity, and Compatriots to Early Passages, Ethics, and Exile, the poetic assemblage shows a sensibility that returns one to the multiple modes and layers of modern African poetics. The volume boasts an urban category under the heading of Cosmopolis. Ismael Hurrah in "Abidjan" in the volume notes April as a time that resuscitates many memories of freedom fighters who fought for the "mutilated remains of Africa." Hurrah's poem also has a continental value for thinking about the need for solidarity and upliftment of Pan-Africanism, as an ideology and framework that can guide Africa away from the plight of the past towards the future of regeneration. Yet, infused in the poem is the urban habitat of Abidjan that Hurrah remembers for "its ringlets of memories" where "dormant thoughts" are stirred.

But "Before we lose ourselves/In this mad harvest of city lights" as Tijan M. Sallah of The Gambia writes in a 2009 Frank Chipasula's edited volume, *Bending the Bow: An Anthology of African Love Poetry*, contemporary anthologies testify to the resurgence of African poetry, even if the African city has remained a marginal concern. The concerted contemporary efforts of Beverley

Nambozo in chronicling new works of African writers in *A Thousand Voices Rising: An Anthology of African Poetry*, followed by the decisive labor of Adedayo Agarau's *Memento,* where new creative poetry avatars exploiting the social platforms and internet have their works recorded must be recognized. Along with the works collected by Agarau, catalogs of 20:35 Africa edited by different new poetry enigmas such as Safia Elhillo and Gbenga Adesina, have also spotlighted the African city image in part. There is strife for social justice in *Sọ̀rọ̀sóke: An #Endsars Anthology* edited by Jumoke Verissimo and James Yeku. Let us quickly state that *Sọ̀rọ̀sóke* emerged as the protesting spirit of the African city of Lagos that marked the springboard for resistance against police brutality and maladministration in Nigeria. All of these anthologies show the journey of African poetry, but where the image of an African city peters in the margin as a trope. We do not aim to create an exhaustive narrative of the profound works of editors that have created different and unique repertoire of works of new faces of African poetry, including *Unbound*, edited by Nduka Otiono and Chibueze Darlington and published in 2024. *African Urban Echoes* simply seeks to fill a gap that we recognize in earlier missions.

Certainly, when we think about African cities, we reflect on the poetry of their mosaic bodies. Odia Ofeimum writes in *Imagination and the City* that, "A city is like a poem. You enter it, and you are into the world of concentrated time." For him, the African urban "surrounds," to use AbdouMaliq Simone's frame, are where, "the secular meets the profane and untold extremities are solved into a common sensibility." The dynamics, beauties, histories, and characters of African cities make them malleable spirits. We are excited by these colors in them and their spontaneity. The African city, we guess, can be fast and uncanny, and can offer the balm when we walk in its faith. The question then is, is the city like a poem? What kind of poem does the city produce, or to reimagine Henri Lefebvre, what kind of city does the poem produce? With an African urban poetic capture, we are thinking of how these urban centers carry the heritage of colonial violence in their walls, roofs, textures, and rhythms. How can we create stories that inspire a lifeworld not of struggles to counter the normative narratives of African urbanity? What other forms of city do we have and hope to live in? There are many questions African cities ask us, that we have not been able to answer. *African Urban Echoes* is our effort to think this through. Because of our attempt to reciprocate the kind gestures of African cities—their languages, resilience, freedoms, and fears—we have resisted the idea of organizing this anthology thematically. We feel if we do so, it may be a disservice to the shocks, and concerns that the poets ask us to think about, especially with the musicality of their works, language, images, and forms.

Likewise, we have refused to provide spatial categories by which some of the works can be enjoyed. As we know, Africa has been partitioned regionally since colonial scramble. There is no attempt in this anthology to sort the works in parts of the West, Southern, North, or East African zones. But we want our readers to feast as they like. It means that if they read the work of a writer from South Africa, the next page may be from a contributor from Nigeria. There are poets in this anthology who communicate their migration experience and their encounters of African cities. In their hands, we feel the tenderness and taste of the African urbanities in a new way. The soft texture of African cities is assured in their songs. Some recall history innovatively. In the work of Tolu Oloruntoba, for example, we find the legacy of colonialism that shaped Lagos as a neoliberal economy. For Tolu, the city is a stage for social mobility where "Labourers on the pyramid scheme/must die/with the secrets in their possession." This evocation connects one to contemporary experiences of Ponzi scheme wealth and multilevel capital development. In "Carthago Delenda Est," ML Kejera notes "Xenocide is patient in the kiln; awaiting the match, piling/wood." This poem frowns against the hate, discrimination, and hardship many migrants within Africa today face.

Collectively, the anthology weaves a new Afropolis relationally. It thinks "with" rather than thinks "of" African cities. We follow the rhythmic voices of poets in the volume advocating for the expansive spirit of the cities and celebrating their resilience against internal and foreign actors. African cities are in the full bloom of their beauty in this volume, as each speaker moves through the urban fragile lines, familiarizing us with their encounter with the city dwellers, and the traffic in the cities' wombs. Most importantly, this anthology insists on diversities, not thinking with the African cities as negative combustion alone, but with polyvalent positive energy. The African cities in this volume have refused to be named as an enduring example of postcolonial chaos. Rather they exemplify the multiple histories, including the serenity that Tade Ipadeola notes in Kampala where music, "piped into the inner folds of night lounges–/Cayenne, Big Mike's, The Alchemist -/a sampler's paradise is the city scene/rouged up to tease the butterflies of night." If we are not writing a utopic postcard of African urban life, we want to think about the risks of walking through the African cities today. Where are the conduits, alleys, and corridors where migrants find shade in African cities? What is our hope? Our hope is that through the intervention of this anthology, we counter, decolonize, and resist the image and assault of Western-formatted interpretations of African cities. Therefore, we have assembled here a medley of voices. Our hope is that through the readers' encounters in this bricolage, new insights are underscored, new voices are recognized, new histories are learnt, and new cities are formed for African futures and our dreams in them.

Jide Salawu	**Rasaq Malik**
Edmonton, Canada	Lincoln, United States

AFRICAN URBAN ECHOES

Migrant Subject

Afua Ansong

I left before I was born
I left in the evening
when my mother was already in America
I left with a bag of corn
to grow in America
I left with sand in my left hand
to build a wall around my house
I left in the wind
and then let the wind know that I was leaving
I left after the flood swept
the people into one room
and dead bodies kept floating into roads
and the dead left too
and became ghosts of this nation
haunting those who left before the whistle called home

Dog Poem

Afua Ansong

Hope and I ate
from the same plate

Fufu and soup.
I offered Hope bones

& Hope sat at my feet.
He was a big brown dog.

In Ghana, we don't keep
dogs on leashes.

They know where to roam,
how to return

to the smell
of their owners,

how to bark
the gates open.

Hope dies
and the replacement

dog accepts his name.
This is when the dreams begin.

I am looking for Hope
in every dog. When I return

to Accra where Hope is killed
by a taxi driver,

I hear my neighbor's dogs.
They don't see each other,

only the sun rise
and the sun set.

When thieves are absent,
the darkness echoes

an orchestra of howls
which wakes the dying

crows who have started
to eat themselves. No one

is innocent in this country.
When the dog show

ends, I slip into the sheets,
& imagine the dogs

stretch their front paws
& smell bougainvillea, sprouting.

Foreigner

Abdullah Olajuwon Adedokun

She looks at me like a crime scene
before the body is found, her eyes—
the detective as she scans my
hand for scars. Rewind. Slow motion.

The laughter is forced, I'm not stupid.
Halfway, she exhales and says *Ahh, Lagos boy.*

She says it so often I remember her face in that,
wide open, pause, forced laughter, *Ahh, Lagos boy.*

Here,
I teach her how to hold her handbag
& in her mind, I become more distant.
I told her not to trust anyone here,
she asks if I'm exempted. Silence.

In all honesty, I'm not.

I have lived here all my life,
but I swear, I have not mastered all the rules.

What can we break, what
can we not break? She asks.

I get to a Danfo and thicken my voice,
I do not want her to see me that way,
I do not want them to see me otherwise.

I glance at her and choose her safety,
as if I can.

Mine Too is Karama

Ber Anena

Somewhere far, a people I know gather
around a steaming tray. Papa lifts the bowl
and gulps the chicken soup. Mama picks
a bony beef and sucks its juicy marrow.

Grandma takes her time gumming the dek
ngor and kwon kal. The little ones giggle
at her lips smudged with shea butter. At 85,
Grandma long stopped envying the teethed.

My tongue runs over my lips, but really,
I have spent the day counting the four
corners of my American apartment.
I imagine each number is a drumbeat,

echoing to the chorus of feet, marking
the turn of another year. I have stood by
the window, listening to fireworks roar
somewhere behind skyscrapers in NYC.

How does the sky get so many colors
in one night? In this city, the ball drops
at midnight and cheers tear past all
the concrete. In Gulu, my people pursue

evil spirits with the noise of clanging pans
first, then they'll chant Happy New Year.
Their laughter reaches me without visas.
My feet twitch to remembered songs.

Candle-lit Folklores

Ber Anena

Now when they ask
where home is, I place
a hand on my chest
and say here – right
here a granary spills
over with laughter
collected at the bonfire,
where Mama's folklore
brings a tortoise back
to life. Home is foundationed in this body,
in the toenail that will stay half-grown because
I struck rocks so many times playing Seven Stones,
in the leg scars carved by spear grass as I learned
to shoot at birds with a catapult like the boys.
Recollections of home swell inside my head, take
me to our thatch-roofed huts and back to this
city, this city with buildings that keep daring
the sky. Home keeps my feet grounded on
the earth where the tipu of my ancestors
convene – watching, even from here – to see
if I'm still unashamed of where I came from.

The Flutist

Chinụa Ezenwa-Ọhaeto

At the bar down the street, there is a woman named Ihemewe
who, every evening, elevates us and our cores with her flute.
The flute's melodies are so marvelous that they never beg for
tactness and keep our drinks flowing until our pockets begin to itch.

It's said that at her birth a strange old man had stopped by
their house, walked in, and without words gifted the flute and left.
The flute has been her play and she has been playing it since growing.
No one knows if this is true, but if it were in another
universe, she would be called Orpheus reincarnate,
for at the bar there has never been a bad evening with her and her flute.

Another story goes that her mother is not her mother,
for Ihemewe was given to the family, that has been looking for a
child for years, by Mami Wota, a spirit who dwells in
the depth of our town's river and is full of baubles.
This river spirit takes anyone who dares listen to her
song into her paradisiacal realm.
Ihemewe's father is one of the men she has held in a trance
with her song. And that is how Ihemewe came to be.

Last month, Ihemewe settled at her usual corner at the
bar and played her flute. But this time, the flute's melodies
were different from what we have ever heard from her.
What caressed our ears was solemn, and told a
story of a daughter who lost her child to the terrors of
the night. I was touched by the melodies that I wondered
if the story was hers, a friend's or someone distant.

I halved my glass of beer and listened on.

In the end, I looked her way and affirmed
I have never heard her play a song with
her flute that didn't carry the beatitudes of
rain and the coreness of her soul.

I Remember You, Mother

Chinụa Ezenwa-Ọhaeto

She thinks I left her behind on leaving the village for the city.
There are things one cannot be taught, he learns himself
like no one taught the Good Samaritan how to be good.

In my head, there are two ends.
One is the village and the other, the city.
The city is where my mother plaits her worries, and
whose prayers are invisible halos above my crown.
This village is where the pines in my chest flag, and sometimes
it opens me up like a man opening a shaken bottle of wine.

Mother,
I remember you in the morning chirps that bloom with the village;
I remember you each time I awoke to the morning noises of the city;
I remember you in the stares of my classmates on walking into my classroom;
I remember you in the smiles of a girl I asked out, and whose laughter
    is clean spring;
I remember you each time I leave school and return to my apartment
to meet my roommate who I think is secretly in love with me;
I remember you in the pages of my worries, keening beside me;
I remember you in the poems I struggle to write and in the fiction I am yet to
    finish;
I remember you when I could not sleep because my throat practiced the alto
    of hunger.
I remember you when I sleep in the night with the dying noises
    of this city.

Mother, do not wear a dimly lit face for
I, your son, am well and, remember you often everywhere
and in this life filled with fire, water and stone;
in this life that holds me at the centre of its cloves.

Hair Products

Dina El Dessouky

Cairo,

I long for you as I long for the hair dye
I won't try for fear of what
I might intentionally cover up.

I long for you as I long for the
Coiffeur's dexterous fingers
wrapping clusters of my hair

like warak 3enab around roller sets,
under the pressure cooker, maqluba
on my head. I long for the surprising cool

of your hot breathy kiss on my scalp
when the lid is flipped and my strands
get a stretch in before their straight is sealed

between iron tongs. I await your Coiffeurs
with impatience as I await
my mother's approval.

Cairo,

I long for you as I long for estranged fathers
and male kin, or uniformed men.
I prefer to revel in your mystery

from a safe watching distance,
behind panes of glass that only Abdul Halim
and chopped onions can steam.

  I long to stomach you
  like the kibde Mama would sear on the skillet,
  winters too cold to air out the house.

  I thirst for you
as shafts of treated hair
thirst for coconut oil—I long to soak you in.

I can't bring myself
to soak you in, can't bring the wind
to throw my caution out

I can't bring myself
to soak you in,
a hair relaxer left in too long.

When I return to you,
the hair I could never part
evenly down the middle
will swoosh to one side
a tattered curtain
  above my eyes

and I may return to uniformed men
on your curling pavement
whom I know nothing about.

I want to love them all awestruck and trusting
like well-off white kids love the cops who bend down
to meet them with police badge stickers at Fourth of July parades,

backlit like angels.
—No,
I want to love you better than that.

I want to love the ones who caved in
for chicken wings
as much as the ones
who lean lazily against talking trees
as much as the ones
who love death metal and consent.

Cairo, baby
hair I'll never slick down
Cowlick of our blood thirsty Baqarah

Allah yi Khaliki
Ya Qahirah

Not because we call you unconquerable
but because we are the wigs
that top your never sunburnt scalp.

Born Location

Emelda Gwitimah

A township boy from Kadoma
born on a goldmine
nothing but the clothes on his back
and the gift of time

a shoe brush and some black polish
"Here's your fifty cents."
Head bent on keeping shoes on shine
every day well spent

...saved enough for a machine,
some leather and some twine
to make the shoes in his own way
and start a clothing line.

A farmer's boy from Kadoma
born by the cotton fields
gave the township boy his funds
to increase the yield,

yards of cloth and leather too
"Look at how we've grown!"
A handshake but no paperwork;
he really should've known

that in the town of Kadoma
the lines were Black or White
no matter who you think you are
the optics must be right.

Made their minds to burn the Plant
the boys broke in at night...
the farmer's boy then turned his back,
the township boy just cried.

A township boy from Kadoma
who thought he'd beat his lack
was dragged right back by enemies.
It hurts more when they're Black.

Oshodi

Gbemisola Adeoti

If you want to dissect the lung of Lagos
take a ride to Oshodi
not minding the smoking coughs of a *danfo*
or the phlegmatic grunts of a *molue*
or the riotous melody of the conductor's ditty.

Oshodi Oke!
Oshodi Isale!

Oshodi is
the theatre of the shoddy and the sloppy
the movie house of the sunny and the superb.
When Oshodi grumbles, Lagos rumbles
like an elephant shot in the gut
by a livid archer in the jungle.

Oshodi is
Iragbeje's house of wonder
where a thousand and four hundred tales
reel out with unending climax
and prolonged denouement
featuring the smart city boy
and the clumsy village bumpkin.

Oshodi was the rock
upon which wonder decided to build its house
on its way from the dome of heaven
to the open glade of the earth...
There,
the thief picks pocket with the purse
and ties the owner's tongue
as he dares not raise alarm
or he risks the wrath of street soldier ants
called Area Boys....
they are the law, its maker and its meaning.

At Oshodi,
the poor in defiance of power and hunger
turn train tracks into shopping malls
for roving souls to shop right or shop left
the train begs for a right of way
when thunderous hooting goes unheeded
by tranced traders and doped buyers.
At night, a 55-star hotel gets erected
in the dinginess of under-bridge.

From Oshodi
there is always a vehicle
dusk or dawn, night or noon
to ferry everyone across tributaries of trouble
to any state of the world –
Mountain of Peace, Island of Prosperity
Creeks of Chaos, Lake of Asperity.

Here,
the phony and the real
are yoked in stable disorder -
fake soldiers, sham policemen
con-artist, swindling state officials
the profiteer and the fraudster
all in pursuit of compromised edge
riding on the horse of teeming credulity.
They are matched in silent conspiracy
against the honest and the decent.

Beneath the flyover - Oshodi Isale
is a flowing river of heads
waved together in common destiny
but facing disparate destinations
they wear anxiety on their foreheads
like a badge, defying the blazing sun.

When Ogun decides to be famished
a vehicle will crush dozens of haggling heads
in one mad orgiastic possession
but beyond the hues and cries of passersby
that sound like interlude in a tele drama
life rolls on with all "busyness" as usual
and Oshodi warbles on, unperturbed.

Oshodi
is the port of moving clinics
borne around by ageing vans
with raucous amplifiers
they hawk disease and death
in unwary currency of health.

It is the meeting point
of those who seek Eldorado
on the map of chance and probability
called *Lotto* and *Baba Ijebu*
It is the assembly
of those who erect their hopes
in hordes of itinerant entertainers
robed as Bishops and General Overseers
they claim to recruit souls for the hereafter
with crumpled Holy Book, broken cross
and ground sweeping cassocks.
In this holy ground of Oshodi,
everything is on sale,
from prayers to curses:
loud prayers for arms that offer alms
silent curses for souls that snub the begging bowl
without dropping a dime.

Here is Oshodi,
where the wonders of Lagos
live, die and resurrect
within a single revolution of the sun.

Gold Coast

Hussain Ahmed

In the name of the children, swinging long sticks over their heads in Jere, beating millets off the stems. I stared at the plate in my hands as the car drove by the mountains and the small huts that kept the road alive to Kaduna. Either of them would have been me before I relocated from the farm, to chase shadows. I learned that chasing is a process, but I have always preferred to escape the chores. In the name of the one who was chased by his own shadows until he settled on a gold coast, the year he returned from hajj. In the name of the one who must return home, to the city that was praised for its gold. In the name of the one whose picture hangs in my father's room, the one who was surrounded by dead men, holding a child that would leave home, just like his ancestors.

Addis Ababa

Hussain Ahmed

From the glass walls,
I saw airplanes taxied –
their wings spread
under Addis Ababa's sky.
There were men in green jackets,
whose voices blurred
the announcements from the speaker
last boarding call!
I stood beside the Christmas tree,
days into the new year,
with a bag the weight of my nostalgia.
In search for a restroom,
I found the chamber
where travelers fellowshipped
under a cloud of smoke.
I found a coffee shop,
where everyone was dressed like pilgrims.

Walls

Hussain Ahmed

In this city,
there are no new houses,

only brothels
built off the old walls.

Whatever smells of blood
is of this city.

We have enough cups
for the dead and the bereaved.

Hargeisa Monologue

Jide Salawu

Hargeisa welcomes you
with its wuthering wind,
carries you with its dry fingers
through the muezzin's voice
over hemispheric dome,
where Maghrebian swears
linger in the air.

Khat kingpins hurry down the street
to give the leaves and twigs a shelf life.
They wake allergic memories:
you are in this continent of your mother
from an ocean-length yard. In Somaliland,
you are visiting Africa from Africa.

Hundreds of ghoulish things
murmur at your window
at Lake Assal and you think
they are disgruntled souls of nomads
pleading for water in a thorn-fenced village.
You think they are your country's fugitives
entering the mouth of the city from the north.

Today is the day of camel milk,
sandy plumes, frankincense dust,
saber-toothed sun, sabayaad,
and desert birds heading
towards the Red Sea. Even if you are hurt,
you must undress your wound slowly.

"Khat kingpins" in "Hargeisa Monologue" was sourced from a 2013 Vice article on Hargeisa by Mark Hay.

Jburg

Jumoke Verissimo

you can love a place so much
    at first sight
then remind yourself to hate
that its geography welcomes you
bemoaning class difference
and stories your kids won't be taught in school.

Lagos Island

Jumoke Verissimo

the stifled air in the market
is not open for discussion
but everyone is engaged
even as
life goes on
in
sun-baked plastic bags
in the open drain
lacking moisture
in
sweaty brows
of flamboyant boys and girls and women
jumping over the gutter

in
algae, spirogyra, and muck
        resting side by side
along with
the laughter and glee
        of bus drivers
        and backdrop of skyscrapers
and dazzling signpost
overlooking potholes
swallowing one tire at a time

once upon a city centre
and its collapsing historic houses

the victory of Victorian architecture
how where
awon boys set up their tent
    festival or carnival
every day is a party day
    life continues

boys and girls and women and men
hurrying to catch a bus
so that the day survives

yesterday didn't survive this island
maybe tomorrow will, maybe it won't
something is always changing in this city
        and it is not the weather.

Oxford Street, Accra

Jumoke Verissimo

clothes and hotels
tourists and owners
tro-tro
billboards and frozen smiles—traders too afraid to frown
fun and fast-food
hunger isn't meant to be a thing if you call the figure right

first time tourists learning to memorise a lifetime story of Africa
on a street that says: *choose your feel*
for this street is a synecdoche
of the unexplored city and its desires

Kitengela Nights

Kọ́lá Túbọ̀sún

Kitengela nights, a freedom flight.
Dry wisps of grass fly by, breaking
With the cold wind of a pregnant night.
Harmattan singes the flesh and mind,
Lungs dotted with dust and rust.

Naïrobi evening. Lights, cold,
And love – ugali and roasted meat,
Nyama choma, in the walled hub
Of a distant home from home:
Then, warmth in the eastern country.

April winds break across my face
In the bust of a fast-moving beast.
We were four – and a few more,
Strangers in a foreign land, alone.
Only love moved, hosted, filled us.

Now, the mind journeys back
In soft bytes of soothing moods:
Dark, homely evening, Kenyan tropics.
Rain and home in a distant place.
Kitengela, you live across from me.

Kenya 2005

Night Road

Kọ́lá Túbọ̀sún

For Ajah. Please swallow softly.

The tyres burning in a side pile
cracking dark sparks into the dry wind
are not a fun bonfire in our autumn,
a happy cauldron of the night
surrounded by wine, weed, and words.

The lines around the block -
stacks of automobiles from end to end
far into where the eyes can't see
are not a collage of a happy convoy
gracing tar for an evening on the town.

The huddled crowd by the roadside
are not a church crowd of proselytes,
nor interested audience of roadside magic.
They may form a wide excited throng
but they don't dance to rhythmic beats.

They are signs of a perilous road:
Tread carefully now: signs to the little city.
Little joys in the tedium of days.
They are a morose crowd at a junction of surrender,
huddled around a freshly minted corpse.

Mawulį

Kordjo Senyo Amenyanoo

ever since Nananom mustered Dutch courage
from the libation we offer with J.H. Henkes schnapps, distilled to taste like Genever,
the Gods have forever taken a French leave;
present everywhere, but here.

777 perfect full moons ago,
the God of Adenta fled to Atlanta;
the God of Dzorwulu migrated to Georgia;
the God of Bubuashie relocated to Boston;
the Gods of Teshie, Nungua and Tema, despised at the taste of Akpeteshie, settled in Texas,
with no T&T;
the Gods of Laterbiokorshie, Bawaleshie and Shiashie now inhabit Lafayette and Seattle
and o!
the God of Alajo could not stand many a police in Minneapolis,
so, He now survives in El Paso.
and they say they are not to blame.
so now, we roam the world
from Kasoa to Kalamazoo
Awoshie to Austin *Alavanyo to*
Alabama
Haatso to Havana
Madina to Madison *Manhyia to Memphis* *Mamfe to Menifee*
Santase to Santa Clarita
Vakpo to Vallejo *Tamale to Temecula*
Jirapa to Jurupa Valley

seeking a chance at living anew or maybe being born again
and if they could be born again,
hoping that they stick to the best pages of life's scrolls and turn no new leaf
as Master Jesuses in Massachusetts.

Hosanna!

Lomé

Kordjo Senyo Amenyanoo

dahomey next door
will yearn for your shore.
coconuts litter around not-so-whitish sands
that surround
the spotless blue sea.
...penguins, pelicans, gulls
sea urchins & seafowls,
tortoises, crabs & rare marines
stroll on your serene saline coast.

and motorbikes toot
about your streets
with treats of Bienvenue along
first-class—second-class—third-class—what-class? roads
of concrete pavement in place of asphalt.

but your markets
are manna grounds
of semi-custom semi-imported goodies
scavenged upon by unwelcomed self-welcomed comers
who go only to come...

back to the dust,
silt & sandy land
from which ebony carved feminine beings
are lilies

that relax my spleen
till my palate gleams
for a longer stay.
in a home away from home,
my mother tongue in a native
non-motherland.

Carthago Delenda Est

M.L. Kejera

I have walked Carthaginian streets older than names of God upturning stones, profaning relics, tearing out pages, fingering lacunae, demanding-asking-pleading why must a city be destroyed? Why would a man punctuate his speeches with war? There are drops-of-red caked over granulated silk; a mother and child sacrificed to borders, stretched across the Sahara. What law-edict-pillar says a city must be spared?

17 kilometers away from Carthage lies Tunis: city of slaves who would be slavers. Here, aged gears grind black into atoms of beigeorangebrowngold. Here, some of my mothers live, here inshallah they will die. Here, school fees are desert crossings. Here, life is worth a bottle of water. Here, I was raised. I could navigate the four kilometers from Lac to Laouina still I am sure of it floating on the sirocco, on whispers of "kahla-gira-gira-kahlouche." Pelted stones hanging in the air would be my stars.

But these are pogrom's streets now, pilgrim. Not for the first time, not for the last, say the bricks of the Grand Synagogue. Flickering street lamps might swoop down after my neck. Yet a question props my mouth open, my mouth stuffed raw with answers, stuffed with diphthongs. Why must a city that I have mourned with be destroyed? Did my wails for Chokri Belaïd and Mohamed Brahmi fail to melt wax-blocked ears? Did I not wrap silence round my throat before processions of the dead? Were the wordsstuckincorpsethroats not la-ilaha-illal-lah but "kahla-gira-gira-kahlouche?" Did I mishear my neighbor yell "La democratie va gagner!" Did he lie, did he yell "kahla-gira-gira-kahlouche?" Did I not stop to smell flowers left by the grateful on tanks?

I am petty now. I call it the Jasmine Revolution as if I was but a tourist, as if I hadn't brushed fist against cheek—cheek against apologetic cheek ya khouya. I have always hated jasmine pettiness odorized in bloom but I would wear a machmoum behind my ear, skip down streets thronged with dogs knowing millennia of sticks hanging in the air guaranteed me protection I am sure of it or have the dogs been taught to bite? Can I no longer walk streets that I am sure of it have led me to where Ibn Khaldun wrote of my people, streets that will lead you to Chaïms Nadir once a pseudonym known to Senghor? Has a pseudonym called me "kahla-gira-gira-kahlouche?"

But what of the children, what of the children who only burn new stars onto night's sky with their lanterns? Was Marie not a child? Did Matyla Dosso not birth a child? Was this not the land of TanitMelqartBa'alHammonMoloch? Xenocide is patient in the kiln, forever awaiting the match, forever piling wood. Bile has scoured any need to tell Fati pseudonym-pixelated-corpse-mother that this city was not always so hungry.

This African skin is not palimpsest to be scratched-sanded-scraped-scoured. Trust us, we have tried. Under thrown stones I have searched-begged for a speck of mnemonic grace for truly why must a city be destroyed? Sand has been sown with the blood-of-a-child, thus my children will learn lies: to love fire, to tighten ox hide red around necks,

to sow salt and reap dust.

The Statesman

Nurain Ọládèjì

The world would rather see hope than just hear its song. And that's why statesmen have to smile.
—Wisława Szyborska

Morning after the governor lost reelection,
I returned to the capital. There was wind
after the rain in the little hours before sunrise;
and the thrill of yesterday failed to spill
into this Sunday. The bus stopped beside
a small bush for a passenger to disembark.
I watched small snails breaking past
the boundaries of bushes, pulling out to feel
the coolness of mud and tarmac.
The passenger, trying to control the chaos
that was his luggage, will never know
he had crushed one under his foot.

We drove deeper into the capital, into an assault
of the governor's face wailing at us from all sides.
Here, in purple t-shirt, shaven, he meant to look
youthful. And here, bright in matching helmet
and reflective jacket, arms folded across his
chest, he meant to show he's hands-on.
And here and here and also here, in lush colors
of agbada, he was gallant and pensive and playful
and I-don't-know-what-he's-trying-to-be-here.

Always in those large eyeglasses and sagging
cheeks, he wore a fixed savior-of-the-people smile.

All that ubiquity and the people still looked away.
Already I saw past the rainy and dry seasons ahead.
I watched the sun lick life out of the governor's faces,
the rains smudging them. And the churches, as the year
trickle out, will pull down what is left to make room.

Osogbo, 2022

Eleme

Obari Gomba

Eleme - even science screams its report
at the people who live there.

A deafening alarm on the level
of benzene.

The pollution of water and air leaves
a people on a tiny thread of time.

Study the mortality tales that are told
by strange diseases in a place
where medicare mocks the seasons.

When they wake up under the harsh light
of gas flares, they open a register of maladies.

A great and brave people live there
and they die there.

And they tell their story. Not of death
only...but of life that always is.

Port Harcourt

Obari Gomba

Port Harcourt - its garden is a cliche
that often grows tired of itself.

What was it before the British took
the land by sleights and cannons?

A home to good people who also lived
their flaws but were far behind
in a game of treachery
that had become Little Europe.

The conquerors pointed their noses at its underbelly
and blasted it into city-hood to service
colonialism which turned everyone
into poor images of the British.

There is still a city there - active in
its expansion, its conurbation,
its toxicity.

But hope is an abiding virtue in the city:
its rivers still run into a mighty ocean;
its dwellers never abandon
the humanity that gives open shores
to all who make their home there.

Ibadan

Obari Gomba

Ibadan – a city of many firsts
and the bards love to sing your praise.

Set where the old and the new embrace
and collide, many come to you
in the seasons of life:
those who seek the stature of grace,
those who read signs on rusty roofs,
those who interpret weather-beaten dreams,
those who nurse their resilience
through the evil forest,
those who return with scars from
their journeys through time.

A city endures where a people endure.

Late Evening In Choba

Omodero David

The din of activity, like rain-song, simmers down
to a soft drizzle of voices hovering in the afterglow.

The loud shimmer of streetlights is but one hour away
from coming alive. Soon, there will be a ceremonious

interchange of trading spots: the pork-meat seller will swap
places with the puff-puff man, the grumpy middle-aged woman

with a truckload of delicacies will leave room for the bend-down-
select clothes sellers whose selling prices drop with the darkening

of the night. Even the madman clutching a sack of scraps, who
seems to be on an endless journey of loneliness, will find rest

in the spot a woman and her kids had sat, earlier, to count how much
the passing world was gracious enough to drop in her plate. At night,

the town is made glorious by the florescent lights of Market Square,
and even more sonorous by the trumpet-blare of freight-loaded trailers

slaloming into the tunnel of tomorrow. Once, my purest joy was to chase
the translucent bubble of wonder as far as the breeze ferried it. Now, I relish

the brightness of the east-west road, watching the briskness of bodies streaming
in a two-way flux; the everydayness of hunger, the persistence of dreams.

Self-Destruction

Okwudili Nebeolisa

Because I had permitted myself
To walk so far that the streets lost
Their familiarity, I refused to ask for help.

The clouds darkened. I ignored the threat
That carried in the lightning that sprinted
Through kilometers of dark gestating clouds.

Nor the brief thrill of static I caught
In my afro. Even the hickory trees
Were shaking, their perfect firewood

Refusing to be merely sacrifice.

I didn't even know when I became
The only person on the street.
I overthink everything; it's my disease.

Maybe, if I stopped, I would come upon
The cobbled streets I had walked through for hours.
Or the row of identical-looking houses.

The light in August changed everything—
It has entered the mind of the sky
And suffocated it with madness.

I Come From A Country Of Wanderers

Patricia Jabbeh Wesley

You know you're a wanderer, when at night
you find yourself
                    leaving,
always leaving.

In your sleep, the plane is flying over West Africa,
the Atlantic, below.

The forestland of West Africa,
                        defiant
against invaders, logging,
annihilation.

Suddenly, you want to get
off the plane,
there, below

is your own country, Liberia, so, why will you let yourself
get down in Accra,
Ghana,
    mother of Africa's independence?
So, you get off the plane,
not sure how.
But they let you drop down
to see your
homeland,

to wander around the edges
of this broken place
to find your father's grave, to go seeking
your mother
whose grave has been moved
to another place.
Even in death,
your people wander.

Your mother's body, taken from its original home,
only the remains that
decades still held,
reburied
to protect her from a country
that eats itself
from the belly button,
inside out.

There you are, wandering in the gutters,
the rocky hills of a city
you have sung forever,
a place that knows
how death smells, the hider of carcasses.
War city.

So, you are wandering among strangers
who may tell your brothers
that you are in town
but then,
you awake.

In bed, in your bedroom,
music, blaring of Jesus
coming again, of rescuing the homeless,
the countryless.

I come from a country of wanderers.
Home-seekers.
People wanderers.

I Am Becoming A Book

Patricia Jabbeh Wesley

My mother never told me I'd turn myself
into a book

as an escape route back to Africa.
Now, I'd like to ask her what book
I was carrying when she pushed me out,
        what poems, what sort of images

ordered my umbilical cords
out on the village floor,

or did I scream out a poem
the way those millipedes that used to crawl
around the hut at night

slithered under our legs while *Iyeeh* told
an endless tale?

The way I live my life, there is a library
        always burrowed under the recesses
of my
being.

The first time I met my husband,
        I was in the middle of books,

pulling books off the library shelves
of a university I needed
more than I needed air.

I wanted this man so bad when I first saw
him from behind library shelves,
his light-light-skinned body
against sunlight.

Tall, Grebo, a bearded face, I thought
he must have walked out of a movie
to ground himself

in that library.

He was not there for a woman.
He said he wanted to give me Jesus
that had been packaged
in a booklet

Christian boys carried around as if
they didn't know
a woman's
soft skin.
But I wanted help finding my books
or finding the roadmap
to a man
my father could not throw
out our door.

But for now, he was good for helping me

find my books, find a thesis sentence,
writing things out
in my notebook.

After all, a man must work
for what he wants,
I was told.

If he helped me do my work,
I'd let him sell his Jesus
to me while I looked at his fine face,
dreamed of the life
after he gave me his Jesus

or until I gave him my ideas of books,
of poetry, of how
a poem curves
into the road,
and becomes the tree under which Jesus
talked all day about love.

So, years later, our first child decided
to come after a long
day at the library with her Mama,
my belly bulging out as I climbed up

old stairways at IU
that day, all Sunday.

Graduate school is like a rocky footpath
into the unknown,

me, taking notes,
writing midterm papers,
the books, talking to me,
the baby kicking as the smell of books,
the smell of old air
from a hundred year old university library.

That next day, after the library,
the baby came, and the man
I met three years earlier in another library
thousands of miles away
in our homeland,
my birthing partner of books
                    and babies,
forever.

They Are Taking My Corn Muffin For Testing

Patricia Jabbeh Wesley

They are taking my corn muffin into security check,
but at the desk, the TSA man
takes one hard look at my ID,
twisting it in the palm of his hand
he stares again,
and another look as I stand there,
    twisting on one old knee
so, my frail knee can ask the questions
I cannot ask.
Somehow, I remind him of the ghost
of the last illegal alien who fled his town.
Somehow, I resemble the crumps
the muffin the luggage drops at the edges
of the carousel after the inspection.

They are taking my corn muffin for testing,
so, the security agent takes out his magic rod,
and I wonder if this is the way an abusive man
takes his rod to whip his sorry wife,
her screams,
dead from afar, as the winds
have taken to secrecy, and will not carry
    her shrill cries across the valleys
where she needs to be heard.
And as she wails that final cry
to death, I wonder if the security man
could hear her cry.

They are taking my corn muffin for testing,
but already, my body has been scanned
down to my buttocks, and my undergarment,
purified, holy, and ready
for the resurrection of "terrorists."
Already, they have placed their radiation
stick over my orange juice,
over my jewelry pouch, opened, and touched
all my body parts, the way a man touches
the body parts of his own woman.
Now I feel my body crawling with worms
and scorpions, centipedes, and snakes.
And I do not care that they brought in a woman
to feel my private parts.

They are taking my corn muffin for testing,
and I am scared of the woman that's patting
down my forbidden places where even God
did not dare to touch during the Creation.
Her hands and her sharp razor eyes
against my delicate African butt, oh,
this ugly world
where we have all become terrorists.
When the security woman sets me free,
I want to weep.
I want to wail my ancestors.
I want to ask her for a place where I can sit
and wail the finalizing of my freedom,
to wail my muffin and my juice
and my jewelry and all the parts of me
that were lost in the screening.
I want to wail because, finally, I have traveled
this far from Africa for this.

Imeko Nocturne

Pamilerin Jacob

My God, the stars. Cities are a curse.
They hide beauty & God, reduce awe

& lore. Here, a single sky glance awakens
the heart, burns more calories than mindless

jogging through city blocks. No muggers here.
No soot-coated walls. Only pure oxygen

from God's mouth himself, filling every lung
like a balloon. Loneliness means nothing here

in the company of crickets & pigeons, hens
& hawks. Every account of the afterlife

is fiction. Yet, I hope
for something similar to this.

Elegy for My Friends and the Streets of Our Dreams

Rasaq Malik Gbolahan

i can’t return to the streets
of these cities & towns
without carrying funeral flowers
to the graves of my dead
and places that unfurl
into memories of years with
my beloveds, our dreams tethered
to the promise of a future that would
arrive without anyone of us dead
or missing. But now i mourn in the
quietude of each night in the absence
of abideen and ridwan, tunde and
islamiyyah and all those whose
graves i have not visited and who
are my beloveds whose graves
i have not visited and whose names
i pronounce each day as i long for
them who once walked the streets
of these cities & towns with me,
them whose hands once held my hands
and whose lives once brightened my life.
Lord, how do i heal the wounds that open
like a door in my heart as i long for my dead?
each day passes and these streets are quiet
in the absence of my beloveds. i miss them.
i miss the salt of their words & the honey

of their laughter on those nights
we carved the future without knowing
that not all of us would be alive when
the future arrives. now i wake up each day
remembering the fragility of this world
where at the end of life we will depart
the familiar streets of cities and towns
where our footprints remain, bearing the stories
of our lives and dreams that will be buried
with us when the tide of death arrives
to voyage us beyond the borders of the world.

Palimpsest

Ridwan Badamasi

Dala rises from the gloom,
its top runs like a crooked spine.
    Charcoal smells wrap around
    the mai kosai's sizzling entrée,
    and bright-eyed young men fill
    the shayi shops.
Old men, veterans of the hard soil, squat
on haunches under the shade of the dogonyaro,
their words unspooling memory like thread,
their teeth kola nut red, faces like cracked
leather. Turare hawkers covered
with dust of the roads lay their wares
on red mats, three dozen scents coiled
in their boxes.
    I count the cattle strolling
    across the road like fat landlords.
    The city is full of shy ghosts.
    Under the glare of the sun,
    this pool of shifting moods,
    bowl of roiling seasons, gleams
    white as bone.

Wednesday Market

Ridwan Badamasi

The sky's about to break, and yet the sun is unrelenting. The Wednesday market sits astride the river, people haggle in ten tongues, ɗandoko flit about with prodigious burdens. Beyond the rice patches, the gentle waters kiss the rough bank. Fishermen cast nets from colorful boats while bare-chested boys dump bronze-colored fish into round raffia baskets. A blind beggar sings at the market's throat, cane clanking. The wind stirs, thunder rumbles, and all eyes turn to the heavens. Only the stray cats keep vigil. What do they hear? Rats scurrying under grimy walkways.

Kofar Kabuga

Ridwan Badamasi

This is a noon where Kano announces itself:
the June heat descending like an oppressive
hand; the sprawl of rooftops written
like headlines; adaidaita sahu
flooding roads like an invasion
of arteries; bazaars at kantin kwari boasting
an encyclopedia of prints. Near Mudassir
a man on the radio sings, *Kano tumbin giwa.*
The overpass at Kabuga winds around
the old city walls, a scrap of ancient fabric.
Oh Kofar Kabuga:
do you remember the hands that—centuries
ago—cut the clay that made you, anointed
you protector of the city—the men that lined
sun-baked bricks up taller than anything
they'd ever seen, fashioning you into
wall, door, lasting sentinel?

Re*_port*

Sarpong Osei Asamoah

In the early 1940s, during World War II, Aircraft parts were shipped to the Takoradi port on the west coast of Ghana from Great Britain.

The flowerless sun sends pollen   with smoke in its tail   into the
    Atlantic
the way twenty-nine fighter planes get shot   down by Berlin

They come crashing like seagull wails   their alarm call
  London calling   *London calling*

Pick up the telephone   pick up the bodies
the decoy   ships sent empty of empire

This secret   the best aircraft parts ever designed
ever languaged   & martyred   ever disappeared   never landed

Takoradi city carried her   fire   in its handful of ocean
    and only told two lies   duty   & friendship.

Landmark May 2023

Salimah Valiani

torrential rain stumping
the Freetown cotton tree

history aflood

Matru 1622
Ma Tenneh cleaved of her teenagers
Titi Georgieta Victor
raked in herself just after

village tribunals 1590s
chiefs and councillors atop rice stores
lance leaning masked advocates
guilty condemned to death sold to best bidders
how many docking
in Mississipi cotton Pernambuco cane

Mano Bonjema Waanje river town
keen on pewter 1506

Benia Daboh two children three nieces
2017 Freetown
flooded jollof stall
drowned sister husband brother in law two fathers mother

Manchester to Freetown 1860
seed gins printed instructions
from Cotton Supply Association to the Bishop and Secretary G.W. Nicol

Bullom 1861
Countess Huntingdon's cotton growing
mission to end the slave trade
along with other cash crops   raiding
forests for over a century

cascading today
in torrential rains

Kwa Thema May 2023

Salimah Valiani

after the cable theft
loadshedding
explosion
the R250/day diggers
were said by some to be
working slowly
to earn more

volunteer diggers came forward
volunteer cooks to feed them

protests
riots
looting
murder
suicide
lots of digging
some power
later

no one spoke
of the missing living wage

Kampala

Tade Ipadeola

At night, this cool city set in deep time
stirs, shape-shifts
from raucous boda-boda men
aiming for impossible escapes
on sun-streaked roads of jousting cars
into a bevy of resplendent ladies.

There is music in Kampala, whispered,
piped into the inner folds of night lounges–
Cayenne, Big Mike's, The Alchemist -
a sampler's paradise is the city scene
rouged up to tease the butterflies of night.

And on the road to Entebbe,
Nalubaale's breath is crisp sillage
seeping into every bud and petal,
every skirt and shirt
that sunrise rinses clean again.

Marrakesh

Tade Ipadeola

Marrakesh is a hummingbird standing still in the sun
A thesis in motion, stilling tongues and dialects
I have watched as her streets dissolve in fun
At night, a Möbius rendering of joy's analects

Leaving Casablanca and its dreams unfurling
With the calligraphy of seismographs, we try
For a trail left by old Almoravids, night calling
The party to a closet of camphor, bracing and dry

As the desert air. The company armed itself fragrantly
With axioms native to the soil, manifest envy
Green as Nigerian passports. For Fez, militantly
As hope, and to Jelloun's country, as memory's envoy

Into modern streets built from bones into plains,
Ancient spoliarium of manifest destinies.
There is poetry here, of neat sculpted quatrains
And jagged, as of the edges of the distant Pyrenees.

Niamey

Tade Ipadeola

Crossing swords with Carbon-14 dates, the museum
Of natural history in Niamey resurrects a dinosaur.
What fed that beast? What prey paid premium
Price? How glad Tenere should now be that power

No longer flows from carnivore diktat? What man
Is there so free from muscled terror now?
Will appetite now fail to gobble what it can?
Though hominid, is one not a lion and the other cow?

A hundred million years and yet the terror still
Of suits in pursuit of the golden sweat
That raises skyscrapers and treasuries of steel,
Dealing in hunger despite wasting wheat.

Millions watch the skeletons of terrors past
They drink their water quietly and eat couscous
Assured that terrors end however long they last
And meekness wins, and nothing different does.

Warri & I

Tanure Ojaide

Warri is no longer the same place to me. In youth
we played games a stuntman won't attempt today.
I somersaulted on top of a disused car tire
and kept my balance firmer than an Olympic gold gymnast.
We sought adventures waiting for accidents to happen
but always did not because of youth's unfailing magic
that assured safety in blindfold devilries on the cliff.

Now bearing the burden of all I gathered
from decades at school, workplace, and travel
if I were to try to somersault on a Caterpillar tire,
would observers not shake their heads in utter disbelief
at a depressed man's choice of suicide in hard times?
If I taunted the cliff, wouldn't I break neck and head
that some would pick away for money-making rituals?

In Okoye Street* a miracle saved curious boys from syphilis.
We envied the outside world that AIDS would ravish
but compelled us to learn the virtues of derided abstinence.
Fame is no longer free in overrated street freak shows.
Notoriety before peers earned such enviable respect
and not Facebook's following cheering what they don't see.
Warri comes to me as I walk away from the place.

Now I am ready to "carry last"* and be triumphant
leaving Warri to its folkloric ways; defeated and happy.

Is it I or Warri that changed beyond recognition?
I am no longer Boma Boy and nobody remembers that stuff
as crafty Wafi is unable to rise to its memorable nickname.
Can I still be a Warri Boy after the countless years that
I have abandoned its wonderful staple to be an itinerant lover?

**Okoye Street: till the 1970s a quarter for prostitutes in Warri.*
**"carry last": from the popular saying, "Warri no dey carry last."*

Benin History

Tanure Ojaide

So that history does not turn into a blind alley,
I visit the fabled moats surrounding Benin.
The footprints of heroic Arhuaran unaccounted for.
Visionary Ominigbo's blood sacrificed for divining truth
untraceable in the traumatized terrain of unfading redness.
Queues of vassal kings with tributes appear only in masks.
Carved for sale, queens and princesses who gave up their lives
so that Benin would forever remain glorious with male obas!
And Ife looms, a large shadow the Oba cannot shake off
at Ododua festival and to affirm the legitimacy of his dynasty.
I travel through centuries of the city's bronzed timescape
bypassing foreign visitors, intruders, and soldiers of fortune
to arrive at today's state capital, coven of political wizards,
haven of sex and human traffickers, den of robbers and assassins
so that history is not forgotten in the silt-filled moats
surrounding immortal Benin. Forever there, glorious!

Seeking Friendship

Tanure Ojaide

The search for friendship brought me here;
a wilderness of two-million stragglers.
I can't make friends of aliens the more I try
to embrace them the more they race away
as much afraid of me as I desire them.
I am also a stranger to them; they believe
I harbor the same perfidy in their hearts.

Traitors fill political circles with their kind;
hence my uncertainty at making friends with those
whose ideology cares for only self and nothing else.
I seek friendship from everyone but I am afraid
of rogues, prostitutes, and dissimulators. By the time
these are extracted from the city, nobody to befriend
except those thriving in virgin wombs or victim graves.

I am afraid of the community in which I seek friendship—
Abuja bustles with Christians and Muslims
but there is no neighborliness in the cramped residence.
The sleepless social media a gang-up incapable of condemning
followers who compliment theft or perjury as wonderful.
I am afraid that where everybody is in a hurry, none will wait
to hear my advocacy of law and order not to talk of ethics.

Nobody will forgive the unbeliever they call a hypocrite
for refusing to be hypnotized into the religious contagion.
I am seeking friendship that does not yet exist—
tricksters and opportunists win hefty awards with craft.
Everybody is setting up one-man companies that are hotbeds
of rituals that instead of bringing capital impoverish them.
Where shall I live to find friends since this is not the place?

Love is 52,625 miles away from Virginia Beach, in my soot-drenched city of Port-Harcourt

Tope Larayetan

Love is in the badly-photoshopped
deliverance posters of churches—

that spring up like waterleaf on the once-blue
gates of Mile 3 and Mile 1 markets

It is in the ariria music solely carried by the
twang of high-pitched lead guitars—

an intermittent hailing of those who stick
currency notes on the foreheads of the singers—

The buses, also painted state blue, croak by
and the conductors call bus stops into the air—

Love is in the "pitakwa, how una see am," 94.1 FM, Wazobia.
It's in the shouts of "abobi," code for my guy, my person.

English is a Limitless Sky

Tope Larayetan

How else to describe this sameness
that could not make us more apart?

The widening of my mouth as I try to explain
okada—red-mud kneaded in the breeze
as one rushes by the corner streets of Ikorodu;
the loud laughter of friends at an outdoor bar,
a child screaming at her mother's spanking.
Rushed waves between friends,
a disappearing smile.
Can you see that commercial motorcycle
wrings its essence?

How do you protect particulars—?
Spun from a fabricated speech
following from parent to child, parent
to child, parent to child.
Their renewed importance
when, driving home on a late night,
an officer says
"Bring out your particulars."
The fumble and fear.
Do you see that car documents do not do justice
to my Nigerian ear?

We are bound with ropes on every side,
borders woven by our adding to this universal tongue.
A word borrowed from here and there,
the many tongues from Babel's wreck.
Our descent into the inexplicable language broth.

How to Love A Port-Harcourt Woman

Tope Larayetan

(Pitakwa)

You are a woman from the garden city.
You spell love in specific terms, in a language dipped in crude oil.

I

First, a lifetime supply of bole, not boli, BOLE. They are not the same.
Bole is how a PH woman visualizes true love. Plantain roasted on an open fire in street corners, adorned by cube-cute yam and potatoes. Bright umbrella stands gleefully blackened by this glorious sacrifice. The well-seasoned fish sizzling to eternity. Your eyes will hurt from the smoke.
I never said it was going to be easy.

II

Who goes dere?
Learn some Pitakwa pidgin. There is the Nigerian pidgin which is alright, I guess
but the Port-Harcourt has a flavor that slides the heaviness off your tongue.
"Abobi, wetin dey work you?" is a rhetorical question.
It is irritating when you do something weird, like we all will.

III

Spray her money by plastering new naira notes on the patterns of her George wrapper and ask the musicians to sing her praises into the crackling microphone to the tune of ariria music.
Let them know that she is no ordinary woman merely because she was born between water and oil rigs.

Finish her with enjoyment.

Lagos Money

Tolu Oloruntoba

Human endeavor
is a clear gin of libation
on the land.
The Portuguese first tried it:
to transact on this coastline
of the continent
        of no particular allegiances.
Elsewhere in another time,
Ernesto Guevara left malarious.

Dead civil engineers
in white fish bellies
bear witness
to the amphibious traders
who spoke in gestures
of commerce
and built this a city
on deeper stilts
than Berger's pylons.

Corporate airs or not,
Lagos and her money
are seldom, or never, parted.
There are more zeroes
than ones in her binary abacus.
She'll pay you hope,
or tales by the shore,
for your trouble.

In Abracadabra Bureau de Change,
you will gather the fundamentals:
that Allen boys will chop your dollar
with sleight of hand.

Labourers on the pyramid scheme
must die
with the secrets in their possession.
So megacity planners
will say, *Èkó ò ní bàjẹ́.*
No, it must not spoil,
and so it's no place for
the illegal, the unbeautiful,
or unvigilant
once their blood runs
dry in the hydraulics.

Investors must renovate
whomever does not fit the decor-
um, take their toll, and paint them
into the whitewash of new estates,
before BBC documentarians,
or the FDI, can see. They are the mortar,
and the bedazzled waterfronts
that seduce you,
the lie they hold.

The three elders will welcome you,
Tarkwa Bay will tell you truth,
but Victoria is always, forever, fabu-
lar. Furtive birds of 6 am,

will recap your objectives
when you wake for work in traffic.
You here, playing for oxygen;
inhaling deep for the plunge
into city blood—
with the black-and-yellow,
of its sweaty-collared platelets
ever borne on slow tides
toward payday—and millennia
of mandatory parking.

You may have heard
of the cashless economy, meaning *you*,
will be cashless in a blink.
Owó Èkó is the once won lottery
paid back in tuition—
for those who believe they can,
and the rest who know they must.

But how many will?

What is the exchange rate
of old dreams for new?

People who tamed the swamps in our city

Uchechukwu Peter Umezurike

Sulphur in the air, the elder totters on his leg of wood,
the elder scrambles for her eyes of glass.

They kill the boy.
His "L" sounds like the "N" in knife.

They kill the girl.
Her skin is as dark as the boy's.

They kill the man.
He sounds almost like the boy.

They kill the woman.
She seems related to the girl.

They torch their houses.
They are not soldiers.

They are not rebels.
Not a random mob.

They dance to the music of bonfires.
The city is hungry again!

As though we're celebrating another festival,
but without the sirens or chorus of tears.

We only watch from the windows,
we prefer sticking a knife in the goat's neck

or cleaving a bird for pepper soup,
but we drink and burp and argue about football,

we laugh at the actress whose lips promise the sky,
we only wish—if only—she were one of us.

We worry that the schools will stay shut.
We fear the price of food might chase the wind.

And when the mayor's voice blares again,
a bloodthirsty anthem declaiming our rights,

we argue for days about lineage—
and guests thriving

like algae in our city,
once a filthy swamp.

We argue about guests from across the hills,
who tamed the swamps we feared were cursed,

who have lived too long like heirs among us,
and we argue as hyenas, spit flying around,

we argue, even as the woman,
who sold fish to us last Friday,

staggers, half-clothed, between tires
and wood burning fiercely on the road,

and we argue while houses,
belonging to people

whose hands we used to hold,
char before new idols.

Lagos Rain

Yeku James

Last night I heard the sound of rain in my sleep.
The roofs in Lawrence welcomed a fury from above;
the wrath of it all flooded a wakeful mind with echoes
of Lagos, that city where petrichor heralds the end
of dryness as rain meeting the thirst of trees mixes
with the aromas of their leaves to spring into life
broken flowers marred by the touch of an angry sun.

The rain in Lagos tricks the clouds; the rain in Lagos
drinks up the unruliness of grace, pouring without
warning nor libations to the ways of a maddening throng,
greeted by the wildness of children cupping their hands
to drink from the puddles mother forbade to enter.

Singing to rescue the trifle of the playground,
a monkey post soon seizes the gaze, a makeshift soccer
net receiving a rushing ball weighed down by a flow
of water that joins in a docile tributary to the street gutter.

On the Island, a Nollywood crew is rushing to save
a camera from a sudden surge. At Tejuosho, market women
defy the downpour, covering their wares like lovers
clinging to each other under a fake rain in a movie scene.

But this shower touches the skin, a real stranger to the flea
market that abhors it; it visits again with patters vibrating

with the warmth of an anxious earth, as a tipsy rainbow
stretching its beauty into the chaos of a city's charm.
Last night a rain in Lagos dared to *japa* into my dream.

The Stars Over Lagos

Yeku James

The stars over Lagos say cryptic things
at night. They beam their smiles over us who
meditate upon the face of the universe like children
under the spell of a stubborn moonbeam.

They say the city does not write about running
brooks, nor script coital lullabies for creaking beds
sung as a refrain to roses dreaming of fire
in a garden of two. They say the city does not sing
seaside laughters, or the pleasures of Jollof beef
melting in the mouth as buttered rice in a plate.

Only the sound of dirges ricocheting off the darker
evenings of endless grief. Only the gongs of gulags,
the sound of chained hands bearing crumbs and hope.

But not so tonight, for the eyes ascend like falconers
soaring to the summit that heralds the glides of
a different muse. Not so, the night of the crimson stars
bestriding the skies like the Colossus of Lagos.
Not so tonight when the stars over us whisper
their names to heads raised to the light above.

Journey

Zada Hanmer

Rounding the corner
past Joburg Theatre,
past the government building, whose name
I've chosen to forget –
it stands on the hill,
a gold filling
in Braam's rotting teeth.

The first of many robots—or traffic lights
if you're not from here—halts the river of cars.
They break unwillingly
against the junction,
waves against the shore.
Lone taxis pass through, shameless,
unaffected by law.

Kotas and vetkoek and boiled eggs
Click's and McDonald's and Steers,
Braam's breath
smells like grease and smog.
The tongue of the road laps us up
as we inch forward
in the morning traffic.

after sunset

Zama Madinana

the city lights
float
across the night

where silver stripped thighs
silence
& burn down
tremendous erections
for a small tariff

on polly street
on nugget street
next to mai mai

in this sordid city
the sleepless streets
give cold hugs to the homeless

Note: This poem was inspired by Johannesburg street life, the homeless and those who have to depend on prostitution to survive.

an ode to braam

Zama madinana

braam rises
to kiss
the unclothed skies

leaving park station
& joubert park
behind

yoruba collides with shona
in biccard street
& a smell of *zol* rules the air

rea vaya bus *amper* hits
the *nyaope* addict
in de korte street

car guards
trying
to catch the fattest worm
outside burning hair salons

bricklayers
hanging from skyscrapers
& alcohol advertisements
blessing giant
billboards

men in suv's
poaching wits students
at kitchener's

the underpaid blacks
consoling themselves
with double shots of hennessey
at bannister hotel

but at night
braam is caught
between hillbrow thighs
quenching sexual thirst

Note: Braamfontein is a very vibrant suburb, full of students and young employees. It is also full of immigrants, so this poem was inspired by that.

Cape of Storms née Good Hope

Brindley J Fortuin

-A storm is brewing-

PING! "Thoughts and prayers to the homeless out in the cold today"
(insert broken heart emoji)

PING! "My heart goes out to those people whose houses flooded"
(insert prayer emoji)
#Blessed
#ThankYouJesus

-After the break-

Tonight, on the 7 o'clock news
hundreds of people homeless as
townships in Cape Town floods
after heavy rains.

Plop, plop, (plot) raindrops in a pot
in bedroom 4
right next to the ensuite bathroom
Sifo (née Sipho) cannot come in today,
the roads are closed.

-After the break-

Tonight, on the 7 o'clock news
hundreds of people protest

service delivery in the Telegraph dubbed
"Best city in the world to visit."
Multiple Roads are blocked by burning tyres
next up: traffic news showing you the best routes home
in time for date night!

PING! "I don't know why *they* must burn anything!"
PING! "They always find something to protest and complain about"
(Insert angry emoji)
(Send status update)

-A storm is brewing-

Collective-riotous-righteous fire
A #Blessed Good Hope for the Cape

birth

alma Simba

today it does not
bare its teeth at me
city lets me hold onto it.
tenderness in the
blazing sun, lorries that
slam down on roads, dates in
glass containers, fruit
spread on open tables, the ghostly
skin of dust that covers the tarmac.

a man hacks at the road
digs for more, picks flesh from bone.
the city can be a hollowed space,
so are most rooms of worship
this one birthed me, an expulsion
from its heaving canals
pathways of drains and
bullfrogs that croak when it rains.
today it does not push me
away when I curl up into it,
lifts its arms up
and holds me in a
lingering embrace does
not bite my wrist, no
blood is drawn. the
bay, spilled honey.

breath

alma Simba

the boats in the port rock on the water
fishermen's nets lay tangled like knotted hair
this city has always been
one of escape, of liberation
of coastal embrace.

there are no moments here,
skirts blow in the wind,
on the beach cross-legged,
the children play with shells.

polished sneakers lined up
along the street wall, sounds
of the mega church praising, coins
jiggling up and down in someone's hands,
the honk of the daladala making
its presence known. a woman in
a white dress walks past, a man
in a white kanzu follows behind her.
11:11 on the dashboard clock

time does not stagnate here
it is punctuated through calls to prayer
throughout the day, the sweeping
of courtyards at dawn, the
last wind that rustles through palms
a promise to etch us into skin call
our names in an empty room.

ayama to ekowe

Emmanuel Anzaku

riding through swali introduced me to a frozen beginning
the cold air was born of the aftermath of a relentless rain

anyama held my pass as if a masculine arm around thin waist
leading, i was led through a shelf of fine maidens who yelled
out of a low-quality lip-hue, wooing me to purchase some bread
yet sko sko winked me warmth

i bidded a safe floating over the water to whom i reckoned 'it's my first time'
with a tease from my fingers feeling her; the nun river
she dazed me with euphoria as if begging my knees to quiver.

angiama took a beating upon her wavy body aroused by the wind
birthing tears a pelting dibbling attempts on our arms
waves were our children following and elegantly
escorting an entrance into the muddy bank of ekowe
guarded by sage canoes ancient issuing me a new story
to share about chance

Abulenla

Jide Badmus

Monster sun melts into a river.
Dusk is silent, soft as cheese.
Lush clouds. Light showers.
Call this a welcome party.

This is where I grew—
beneath this savannah sky.
The air is green. Traffic is lean.
This city offers a blank cheque
of serenity & nostalgia.

The distance between Sawmill
& Tipper Garage seems shorter
than I remember. Does an aging
city shrink into its own bones?
Old luxury mansions now stand
nondescript—out of place,
out of grace.

I find laughter in the ribs of time
revisiting old crime scenes—
retrieving kiss crumbs &
cinders of poolside eros
—tooth-picking memories
of museum Ponmo &
Kwara Hotel suya.

Abulenla, the place of modern furniture, is still an old bungalow, unperturbed by the construction around it—a perfect mascot for this big small community.

Idi Aba

Jide Badmus

Your voice is alien to my ears—
natural, guttural croaks of toads
& chirps of crickets.
Your palms, like aqueous balm,
stroke my skin & heal
each stripe of Lagos stress.
Your primordial scenery is visual impetus—
swollen earth & cleavages beckon to me.
Your eyes are green
& your feet are dusty brown—
fire for my muse!

there is a place doves gather

Joseph Hope

to die under large rocks, their bones a tattoo
on the rugged surface, glorified like a monarch's tomb.
here birds succumb to the beats of worms
and peck continuously on the tree of death until a song
is born to the children of men.
on a hill far away
stands an old rugged town,
a city on a hill can still be hidden by soot,
dark soot from the breath of dragons,
or farts from the anus of the government that loves blood
more than water. E~NU~GU: who broke you so like a spineless vertebrate,
and planted a perennial crop of grief somewhere deep in your eroded heart?
who bled you dry my sacred hills? udi hills sang like saints in a lion's den,
like weeping women in a slave ship bound for hell.
and capitalists danced to her elegy, their breasts and
nutsacks jingling like a tambourine.
this place of beauty stands
on the bones of perished workers, trapped underneath rocks
like arthritis in the joints of an old man. black coal, blood coal, blood money
in the pockets of vile capitalists. ancient city, your doves shall fly again.
I'll follow them, the trails, and even stop at the ancient creaks.
bones don't stay buried forever, ask karma!
history have tried and failed to erode your hills,
to bury you in the ruins of wrong metaphors.
gods are people who refuse to die. fly, fly, fly, my city doves.

Minna

Ojo Olumide Emmanuel

slanted by hills to the east
heaving with flurries
i know this city like
the rumbling worms in my belly
harsh with harmattan in January
blasting lips in February
heavy with sunshine in March
and all year round it yells and coos
envelops you as though the heavens
have found a perching floor
only to betray you with harsh winds
and body-roasting sunshine.
this city holds a sickle to the necks
of its occupants once in a fortnight
when angwan daji and limawa hoodlums
collide over foolish disparities and
brandish streets with weapons
stealing the souls of the street
as daylight dissolves into a mirage of inactivity.
this city- again, makes you soar
softens your heart with its delicate beauty
and a warmth of people your soul entwines with
and with the many poems they conceive in your soul
as you raft through the dilemma of making it a home
forever or resting your eyelids on a forward gaze.

i am a junction in my city

Osagiede Best

the highlife songs that fill night tricycles—blue lights on soaked skies;
the gin-soaked herbal roots that fill empty cans of water,
hawked about by middle-aged women,
 retired sex workers
along the intestines of bus parks;

the northern men dollar cutting, gold against grey kaftans;
a lad [bus conducting] holding his beltless trousers by the loop
as it sags below the knees;

the 'Ogun dey kill your papa,'
the drivers' mouths spit on the windshields of other drivers' ears;
& the mothers promising whimpering children dirty slaps

part the air.

& where i am in all of this?
looking for where life wants me to climb her.

sometimes that
i am running,
everyone else is running.

when the sky leaks,
the bus bride price goes up;
drivers, red-eyed, tell us the
engine's food is expensive.

these days are just not brief;
some mornings, on neckties,
holding obese bibles,
pour mispronounced English tongues on mics.

you hear,
'since the bus is full,
can't we lap?'
can't one adult human sit on another's lap?

if not,
can't someone sit on the neck of this distant eater?
how much of the hotness of the attachment can the buttocks take?

yet we live: laugh, work, fight, eat, sex & rest,
right after we have bled.

my city's ulcer

Osagiede Best

they say you do not eat with forks and knives;

when a seed falls from the rich's table, you scurry; you know spaghetti eats money, & two little cups of rice buy big cash.

inside this city, at least two beggars are tied to the hem of a shirt before the body that wears it drops undead from a bus.

that to make eba, one has to let the spring boil & then pour it into a deep valley before cassava dust is introduced.
countryman said he was so hungry he could cry, for the spoons were scratching their teeth on indifferent ceramic plates with ulcerous cracks.

Wild Petal

Servio Gbadamosi

There are little wild flowers
blooming by the stream that
cuts the footpath from work

To home or home to work
just before the mechanic's shed,
right after the welder's workshop.

Surviving this city pushes me
past the patch, never sparing
a moment to stare until this

Evening when I saw a man
stagger away from the gin joint
crushing a petal and then another.

The voices of the splintered flowers
were dwarfed by the drunk's grunts—
bits of shredded hibiscus lay strewn

On the path like the hopes my heart has
borne these years, of me and this dark
country making love to a moonlit wind.

How many more days of sunlight
how many nights of roots reaching
deeper into the receding water table

Will right this wrong? How many more
days of false blooming, until the
violator returns like market days...

Oke Oore

Sodiq Alabi

Once I was walking towards Oke Oore
The sun was blasting its rage, a laser,
At the head of the hill
The refraction was blinding
In the seconds before gaze was averted
I saw beauty waving rays at me.

Oke Oore welcomed mẹ in her arms
I sat at the base of the hill
A robust bulge casting shadow over me
I watched as people came and left
Christians in search of miracle
Children running barefoot on the hot surface
The muadhins at nearby mosques called me to Asr
A new asphalt road took people up and down the street
I thought to myself: This is home.

I was a prodigal returning home.

Odo Oba, at the other edge of town, welcomed me
I had stopped at a fancy new hotel by the river
Its water, brown from earth and pollution, moved slowly
The vegetation by its sides
Serving as the conductor of its journey
Odo Oba looked harmless, but I knew better.

I was a prodigal returning.

As I made my way through a plate of eki[1],
And snacked on robo[2]
I stared at the goddess that had saved my ancestors
Time and time again.
Iwo, Geri mallami, tucked away safely from wars
That devastated Yorùbá country for two centuries

I was a prodigal returning home.

At Odo Oba, I saw a parrot pause to quench his thirst
Iwo, Geri Mallami, where all came to kill their ignorance.
Sit, here, learn jurisprudence in the sing-song voice of Ile Amin.
Iwo, of the great diplomacy of Momodu Lamuye
Oba A-wa-ye-ai-ku[3], envoy of peace.

I was a prodigal returning home.

And it was peace I felt
Walking down the streets from Òkè Àdán
Through Láìtó, Kájọlà, down to Òkè Ọlá
Through Òkè Afọ́ via Yáfóyè, up Hospital Road,
And curving in by Professor Ládipọ̀'s House
Snaking through shortcuts to Òkè Óòré
Safe from endless traffic of big cities that often raced hearts.

I was a prodigal returning home.

In Iwo, I had time to breathe and trace
The memories of my childhood and the dreams of my future,
While I navigated the ruins of abandoned family houses
And the new buildings of those who stayed
While we left
Searching for things that were never missing.

1 *Eki- a delicious meal made from black-eyed beans*

2 *Robo- a round snack made from groundnut and melon*

3 *A-wa-ye-ai-ku (roughly translates to "no one lives forever)- nickname for the longest reigning Oluwo of Iwo Oba Ayinla Lamuye*

Illy

Temiloluwa Okanmiyo Oluyemi

I.
The sun sets in this city
& everything stills
So, you lose grip of the things that are trying to unmake you

II.
Here, you get the strength to fight again
It's in the calmness with which she bustles—
Affirmation that there is culture beneath this soil
You unearth it, draw power from it

III.
The music of this city stays
It follows you everywhere you go
It's melody proclaims peace
This peace envelopes you

IV.
The muezzin calls for maghrib
& so you walk
Past the central mosque
Into the beauty of home

'An ode to my parents'

Fatma Latif

these longer nights are spent in the company of old picture frames. traveling down each
road of reflection, warmed with the welcoming scents of my mother's favorite: sandalwood.

i can still remember.

the lime and lemon garden in the backyard, where i spent the better halves of my childhood
summers, splashing waters everywhere, hiding from the sun in an inflatable pool.

humming the longings of ray charles, here i am. revisited with memories of my father
through a favorite of his. and i can still remember,

the playful and silly dances he reserved only for my laughters.

rediscovering my parents through the hopeful smiles of younger love,

through the histories weaved to make a home to home us.

through my mother's rare and precious reveals, tracing her heart's teenaged tales.

in the face of a violent erasure, in an unforgiving, unmistakably prejudiced world, i have
been trying to hold onto my memories of home.

but it's the proud journeys i think of. the lines of ancestry that shaped my parents, and all the
parts of me mirroring the parts of them, mirroring parts of these communities.

there is a certain remedy in old family photographs. a reminder on the days where i feel
more like a lost branch battling winds of indifference.

i am stronger, and more resilient than this current. i have richer worlds of heritage, bigger
worlds of beauty, love and kindness behind me.

i am my mother's childlike hope, balanced tenderly with my father's realism.

i have deeper roots that will always call after me. never will i allow this world to silence them.

i will keep reminding myself, over and over, to continue to unearth and reconnect. to reaffirm my belonging to this skin,

lest i forget to stand firmly and carry the weight of this name.

The City's Backdoor

Rahma Jimoh

I do not plead to survive
this state with its colonizer's tooth.
I'll leave instead for other pastures.

Call me a prodigal running, but
I am not. My mind's eye
can envision the future already.

It is true that you do not see you
until you step out of your skin.
I've strived so hard to love here,

even with the desecration. Reminds
me of the innocent boy from the tutorials
before he wore a Yoruba man's crest.

Look, I do not know how to comfort
what I do not know how to love,
or what has decided to be unloved.

This country has killed me daily
& my body is weary from dying.
I try, I want to fall in love with her

but everytime, I fall flat on my dreams.
Yesterday picked the remnants of
my dreams & took a French leave

through the city's back door.
Again, my memory ricochets to the boy
from college, how he broke me.

Zone 4

Denja Abdullahi

Flushed faces, tempting cleavages, too-sweet smiles,
Melodious backsides jostling for attention,
Coquettish eyes x-rays bulging pockets and groins,
Shish kebab wafts meaty spices from opposite lanes,
The Mallams re-arrange slices of dripping fruits.
From a 4 wheeler, the voyeur peeps
Undecided on the juiciest of them all:
Welcome to Zone 4!

Khaleelur Rumi

Abdulrosheed Oladipupo Fasasi

What do you think becomes of Shams, a place of stars? Or
A garden of saints beside a bar? City has a way of burning the scope of martyrdom;

Sound of bell, the frontage of sea blessed with lusts of pearls,
Cry of donkeys and markets of flirts; bartering flesh for sweetness,

When it rains in the city; it is a god's wish for it to flood,
Everyone knows where Jide stays, you know his addiction to coffee,
And his obsession for stumps and new olives, a poet of winter,

Minstrel of bodies, a pope of Verona. Say; the city has a way of overcoming
A poet, an addict of a thing, a room of exiles, gods inventing new names,

Faulting every Eve's choice. An Agbowó of boys who see beyond.
The biology of things. A Pragma that steals Shams from his Khaleel,

When the city becomes your inspiration, poems become
A hymn of adornment and solitude becomes unworthy

Of all things. A poet who writes from the city cannot be
A judge of Shams and the aches of his soulmate.

Benue's Call through Makurdi to Mhambe

S. Su'eddie Vershima Agema

Echoes of home summon from afar

We answer and tread the tarred paths
Abuja fades to Keffi, Akwanga, Lafia and Makurdi
We behold barren landscapes bereft of trees
Ancient saluting sentinels now only rooted to our memories

Past the River Benue, whispering Ikyarem's tale
And the eternal silence of many souls thrown for Biafra's cause
We pass North Bank's new bridge to Wurukum's basket
Our eyes feast on the sights as pounded yam tag teams pocho and okro
At a temporary banquet that settles stomachs

As more pounding summons others, we rise to the sound
Of our homeland's song:

Somewhere, the kakaaki resounds and people hail
Bodies bend, twist, and writhe to the rhythm of swange and girinya
Dances of glory and anticipation as the wind strums a lute to command.

As the paths lead on to Wanune, Gboko and on
You witness the harsh plains, notating discordant tunes
The crooked roads and sounds conduct a cacophonous composition
That become a symphony of my remembrance
Aiding my eyes to lost times with past joys
As the gallops knot your sanity, like jarring percussions
I dance to its every bump, a man lost in a forgotten time capsule.

Within the vault of our minds, thoughts conduct their own orchestra,
Memory vibrates like strings,
—echoing Father's protective promise, a soothing refrain,
—Aunty Pat's embrace, another stanza sang in a minor key,
Laughing away the worries of the journey, a pause in our shared song.

Now, they rest beneath concrete mounds in our *tse*, the *agbo ile*

My heart guides my smile to Makurdi, Gboko, Ihugh
Then Mhambe, the cadence of home
Previous pathway, an unpolished opus, an unrefined symphony,
Slowly, I shape it, my baton guiding life's score,
Through journeys repeated over and over, cascading to a crescendo,
Until we too find our rest beneath the quietude of concrete mounds.

The Patriot

Dami Ajayi

The squirrel's singed pate fits the plate
as a propitiation for fate's palate;
the patriot, who chose land over love over fawning,
stands with unease, hoisting an awning

of a roadside stall in Yaba; his ears adjacent
to the diaphragm of the record store's speaker
whilst lightning scuttled skies otherwise translucent
& a stallkeeper prises her billowing skirt from the winds,

ladle in hand, warmth in her heart,
gratitude for the dutiful patriot's bravery
& her graceful movements a small dance,
a stooped routine of tending gravy.

Years later, a British passport fits the hand
toiling that stormy evening, now blurry
a worthy reward, a sword on a shoulder blade
like the seething soup of turkey.

Acknowledgements

This work took us several months to conceive. It began on a trivial note in 2022 when Rasaq and I were on the phone chatting on mundane things. Then it slipped into deeper conversation about African cities and their viscerality. I noted for Rasaq how quickly much of poetry around African cities appears in fragments in local and international journals by old and new voices in Africa. These poems were compelling enough, but their power, force, and voltage will be more generative if anthologized. In fact, new images of Africa and its cities, allures, beauties, and dissonances can be appreciated in a work like this.

So, the idea of *African Urban Echoes* started. Many people have been supportive of this project from the inception. We must thank our publisher, Bibi Ukonu, for pushing the inspiration far beyond expected horizons. He was willing to dedicate his editorial and publishing resources to a vital project. He has been one of the unmatched blessings to African literature, providing a platform for new writers. Through Bibi's Griots Lounge, our faith solidified that this was an achievable project. We appreciate Jumoke Verissimo for her support and fine words. It was like listening to the inner voice in our heads. Our spirit was uplifted by Kola Tubosun, publisher of *OlongoAfrica*, who has been an unrepentant energizer throughout the anthologizing process and the publicity.

We recognize the efforts of friends that help us drive creative humanities forward in an innovative way. We are reminded of several deliberations of Tosin Gbogi, Uchechukwu Peter Umezurike, Hussain Ahmed, Arthur Anyaduba, Ifeoluwa Adeniyi, Shola Adenekan, and others who accept this call as necessary and path-charting. We are grateful to Aneihi Edoho, Ukamaka Olisakwe, Troy

Onyango, Otosirieze, Adedayo Agarau, and many others who found it worthy to promote the call on Twitter, Instagram, Facebook and other social media handles. Thank you Maria Bustillo, and the entire household of Brick House and Flaming Hydra for your publicity.

We are indebted to the contributors to this volume, some of whom are mentors and friends. Their literary companionship and comradeship in poetry is quite emulatable and has kept us this far. We thank our partners for their support and encouragement in making this project a reality.

Our endless thanks also go to Prof. Michael Bucknor of University of Alberta for their constructive insights on the preface and the exposure it carries for the corpus of African poetry. Professor Nathan Suhr-Sytsma of Emory University for his constructive suggestions on making this anthology one of the best poetry archives and praiseworthy. Our arrival at the generative poetry archive on African cities may not have been possible without much support from Professor Cajetan Iheka of Yale University, Professor Sussana Sacks of Howard University, Professor Matthew Shenoda of Brown University, and Upile Chisala. We are excited by your generous words.

Born in small towns, Rasaq and I have spent part of our lives in the cities. Rasaq on the one hand spent a huge part of his time in Ibadan as a graduate student at the University premises, sifting through different poetry activities, while I spent my time in the ancient city of Ife, where I spent my time learning about the African greats in poetry. Collectively, our lives have been linked strongly to that African arch urban space: Lagos. We think with the African cities, and we thank them for the echoes We are glad for the hopes and lights in them.

Contributors

ABDULLAH OLAJUWON ADEDOKUN is a Nigerian teen writer who was born and raised in the suburbs of Lagos. His works appear in Eunoia review, Brittle Paper, Rusted Radishes, and Writers Space Africa among others. He is a Foyle Young Poet, a second runner-up for the Leonard L. Milberg '53 High School Poetry Prize and a winner of the Barjeel international poetry contest.

AFUA ANSONG, Assistant Professor of Africana Studies at the University of Rhode Island, holds a Ph.D. in English Literature and Creative Writing and an MBA from URI. She completed a postdoctoral fellowship at Mt. Holyoke College and her full-length poetry collection "I buried [her] in a field of lemon-grass" was a 2023 National Poetry Series finalist. She is also the founder of the Adinkra Project. An accomplished poet, she authored chapbooks including *Black Ballad* (Bull City Press, 2022), *Try Kissing God* (Akashic, 2020), and *American Mercy* (Finishing Line Press, 2019). Afua is also the founder of the Adinkra Poetry Prize, which supports emerging poets in Ghana. Explore her work at afuasong.com.

ALMA SIMBA is a writer and historian interested in the potentials and failures of words in capturing the human experience. Her area of interest is ancestral heritage, memory, and histories of marginalised identities. Alma recently completed her MA in History at The University of Dar es Salaam with a focus on Tanzanian heritage housed in Germany. She was a 'Sensitive Provenances' Research Fellow at The University of Göttingen in 2022 and is part of the Ajabu Ajabu audio-visual collective in Dar es Salaam, Tanzania.

AMENYEANU KORDJO SENYO MARTIN taps from the indigenous oral traditions of Ghana and his native Togo and finds his voice in the written forms of free verse. Coming from the academic background of mathematical & actuarial sciences, he has a massive inherent zest for words. He writes poetry under the pseudonym Kordjo Zankeli.

BER ANENA is a Ugandan writer. Her poetry and prose have been published in *The Atlantic, adda, Off Assignment, Black Warrior Review*, The Caine Prize anthology, *Brittle Paper, The Plentitudes*, New Daughters of Africa anthology, *The Kalahari Review*, among others. She's a Ph.D. student in English (Creative Writing) at the University of Nebraska-Lincoln. Anena obtained an M.F.A. Writing degree from Columbia University in New York, an M.A. in Human Rights, and a B.A. in Mass Communication from Makerere University in Uganda. Her debut poetry collection, *A Nation in Labor*, won the Wole Soyinka Prize for Literature in Africa in 2018.

BRINDLEY J FORTUIN is a final year doctoral researcher at the University of Edinburgh. Their work explores black and queer embodiment and spatiality within the trans* and gender nonconforming communities of Cape Town, South Africa. They completed their undergraduate degree (Hons) in Sociology, Politics and Religious Studies at the University of Cape Town.

CHINUA EZENWA-OHAETO (@ChinuaEzenwa) lives in Lincoln, NE where he is completing his Ph.D. in English at the University of Nebraska-Lincoln with a focus on Creative Writing (poetry). His works have appeared in *Isele Magazine, AFREADA, Poet Lore, Massachusetts Review, Frontier, Palette, Malahat Review, The Common, Southword Magazine, Vallum, Mud Season Review, Salamander, Notre Dame, Anmly, Up the Staircase Quarterly, Spectacle Magazine, Ruminate* and elsewhere. His debut collection, *The Naming*, is forthcoming in Fall 2025 from the University of Nebraska Press.

DAMI AJAYI is a psychiatrist and writer of Yoruba descent. He studied Medicine and Surgery at Obafemi Awolowo University, Ile-Ife, Nigeria where he co-founded the literary magazine, Saraba. His first volume of poems, *Clinical Blues*, longlisted for the Melita Hume Prize and the Wole Soyinka Prize for Literature in Africa. His second volume of poems, *A Woman's Body is a Country*, was a finalist for the Glenna Luschei Prize. His critical reviews of music, film and popular culture have appeared in Chimurenga Chronic, Guardian UK, The Africa Report, Lost in Lagos Magazine, The Elephant, Bakwa Magazine, Afropolitan Vibes Magazine and also in translation in Das Goethe (a Die Ziet supplement).

DENJA ABDULLAHI is a Nigerian poet, dramatist, playwright, arts administrator and culture technocrat. He has 13 published books to his credit ranging from collections of poetry, plays , collected interviews on arts and cultural administration and co-edited scholarly texts. Denja Abdullahi, apart from lecturing and other public service vocations, has also practiced active journalism with The News/A.M News/Tempo group in Lagos, Nigeria in the 90s. Denja Abdullahi , is presently a Director with the National Council for Arts and Culture, Abuja, Nigeria He is the immediate past President of the Association of Nigerian Authors (ANA) between 2015-2019 and a UNESCO-certified global facilitator on the Intangible Cultural Heritage of Humanity.

DINA EL DESSOUKY was born in Hamburg to Egyptian parents from Cairo and immigrated to the United States at age three. El Dessouky teaches writing at the University of California, Santa Cruz, where she completed her doctorate in literature. Her poetry chapbook, "From the Zabbala's Cart" is part of *New-Generation African Poets: A Chapbook Box Set (Sita)* (Akashic Books, 2019).

EA ANZAKU was born in maiduguri, but the boko haram threat prompted his family's relocation to abuja where he now lives. anzaku is a bookkeeper, customer management specialist, spoken word poet, and a getting-stuff-done advocate. his spontaneous nature led him to go into hyperfocus in 2017 causing him to take on a 365-day poetry challenge which was successfully completed in 2018. '*ayama to ekowe*' captures his first-time experiences in bayelsa state, where he feels at home. his poems '*mek wota get ai*' and 'pilgrim' have been featured in the poets in nigeria (PIN) quarterly journal.

EMELDA N. GWITIMAH is a fiction author originally from Bulawayo, Zimbabwe. She holds an MFA in Writing and Publishing from the Vermont College of Fine Arts. Her stories "*The Hog*" and "*The Jacaranda Letter" were* published in the Intwasa Short Story Anthology. Her other work has appeared in The AKE Review, Bambazonke Magazine, The Willowherb Review, The Post Online Journal and in the inaugural issue of the Ipikai Journal. Her poems have been longlisted in the African Writers Awards and the Our Stories Redefined 2023 Poetry anthology. You can follow her on Twitter (X) @bellaemelda. She currently resides in Canada.

FASASI ABDULROSHEED OLADIPUPO is a Nigerian poet and the author of a micro-chapbook "Sidratul Muntaha" (*Ghost City Press*, 2022). His poetry has been nominated for Pushcart Prize, Best of the Net and Best New Poet anthology. His work has been published or forthcoming at; *Poetry South, Oakland Arts Review, Carolina Muse, ROOM, Santa Ana River Review, Ambit Magazine, Southern Humanities Review, Oxford Review of Books, Olongo Africa, Stand Magazine, Louisiana Literature, GASHER Journal* and elsewhere.

FATMA LATIF is an aspiring writer from Sudan with two internationally published poems to her track. She began writing in the eighth grade. Penning stories and sentiments in her native language, when she turned 18 years of age, she created a personal blog as a birthday gift to herself as a space to actively post. Fatma's writing journey marks the honest unravelling of a woman-becoming. Fascinated with the human condition, she tailors each piece as a conversation and a testimonial, a liberating declaration of a life that is lived and valued deeply.

GBEMISOLA ADEOTI is the author of Naked Soles (poems), Voices Offstage: Nigerian Dramatists on Drama and Politics, Aesthetics of Adaptation in Contemporary Nigerian Drama, Nigerian Video Films in Yoruba, Editor of Muse and Mimesis: Critical Perspectives on Ahmed Yerima's Drama, African Literature and the Future and Inside African Forests: Critical Perspectives on the Novels of D. O. Fagunwa. He was a British Academy Visiting Fellow at the Workshop Theatre, School of English, University of Leeds, United Kingdom in 2008 and a Postdoctoral Fellow of the African Humanities Program from 2009-2010. He was the Director, Institute of Cultural Studies (2011-2015) and Dean, Faculty of Arts, Obafemi Awolowo University, Ile Ife (2015-2019).

HOPE JOSEPH is an essayist, fictionist, and poet. He writes from Nigeria, West Africa. His works are forthcoming or already published in *Notre Dame, Christian Science Monitor, Augur, Stormbird, SolarPunk, Riddlebird, Reckoning, The Sunlight Press, Wizard In Space, Curio Cabinet, Speculative City, Timber Ghost Press, IBUA, SprinNG, Evening Street Press, Zoetic Press, Spill words, Writers Space Africa*, and more. His poem was shortlisted for the IBUA: bold continental call 2022. He's a reader for reckoning press. He was a fellow in the 2021 SprinNG Writing Fellowship. He tweets @ItzJoe9 & IG: _hope_joseph_writes website: https://mssg.me/3j5ka.

JIDE BADMUS is an engineer, a poet inspired by beauty and destruction; he believes that things in ruins were once beautiful. He is the author of four books including Obaluaye (FlowerSong Press, 2022) and What Do I Call My Love for Your Body (Roaring Lion Newcastle, 2022). Badmus has curated and edited several anthologies, and his poems have appeared in Agbowo, The Muse, Maroko, Kreative Diadem, Jalada Africa, Sub-Saharan, Afrocritik, Black Bough Poetry Anthology and elsewhere. He is founder of INKspiredNG, Poetry Editor for Con-scio Magazine, a mentor in the SprinNG Fellowship.

JAMES YÉKÚ, recipient of the Alexander von Humboldt Fellowship, is an Associate Professor of African and African-American studies at the University of Kansas where he teaches African literature, and digital cultures. He is the author of *Cultural Netizenship: Social Media, Popular Culture, and Performance in Nigeria* (Indiana University Press, 2022) and the poetry collection *Where The Baedeker Leads*. His most recent publications are *Ambivalent Encounters and Other Essays* (Griots Lounge, 2024) and the forthcoming monograph, *The Algorithmic Age of Personality: African Literature and Cancel Culture* (Michigan State University Press, 2025).

JUMOKE VERISSIMO is an Assistant Professor in the Department of English. She teaches and teaches in the areas of creative writing (poetry, fiction, and non-fiction). Her scholarship extends to African literary criticism and literature, memory studies, traumatic affect and research creation. She is the author of two poetry collections (*I am memory* and *The Birth of Illusion*); a novel (*A Small Silence*); and a children's book (*Aduke and the Moon's Hidden Secret*), which she also translated into Yoruba. She is co-editor of *Sọ̀rọ̀sókè*, an anthology on police brutality in Nigeria. She is completing work on a novel and an essay collection titled "Elliptical Imaginings," in which she examines the ellipsis as a conceptual framework for her writing practice.

KỌLA TÚBỌSÚN is a Nigerian linguist, editor, travel writer, and scholar. His works have been published in African Writer, Aké Review, Brittle Paper, International Literary Quarterly, Jalada, Popula, Saraba Magazine, etc. In 2016, he became the first African to be given the Premio Ostana, a prize given for work in indigenous language advocacy. Tubosun is the brain behind YorubaName.com, a first crowdsourced multimedia dictionary of Yorùbá names. He has been translated to Italian and Korean, and currently works as a freelance lexicographer with Oxford University Press, UK. His collection of poetry *Edwardsville by Heart* was published in November 2016 by Wisdom's Bottom Press, UK.

ML KEJERA is a Gambian writer based in Illinois who was raised in Senegal, Saudi Arabia, and Tunisia. He has been shortlisted for the Commonwealth Short Story Prize and is a recipient of the Miles Morland Writing Scholarship for his in-progress novel, *The Dictator's Eidolon*. His work can be found in *The Nation, adda, and LA Review of Books.*

NURAIN ỌLÁDÈJÌ is a writer, editor, and a reluctant resident of Lagos, Nigeria. His work has appeared or is forthcoming in *Poetry Wales*, *Olongo Africa*, *Transition*, *Acumen*, and elsewhere.

OBARI GOMBA (PhD), an Honorary Fellow in Writing of the University of Iowa (USA) and the Associate Dean of Humanities at the University of Port Harcourt, has been the TORCH Global South Visiting Professor and Visiting Fellow at All Souls College, University of Oxford (UK). He is a recipient of Rivers ANA Distinguished Writer Award and a two-time winner of both the Best Literary Artiste Award and the First Prize for Drama of the English Association of the University of Nigeria, Nsukka. His award-winning works include *The Lilt of the Rebel, Guerrilla Post*, *For Every Homeland*, *Thunder Protocol*, and *Length of Eyes*. He curated an anthology featuring 35 writers from 33 countries, entitled *A Piece of Daily Life*, for the International Writing Program of the University of Iowa (USA) in 2016.

OJO OLUMIDE EMMANUEL is a Nigerian Poet and Book Editor. He is the author of the Poetry Chapbook "Supplication For Years in Sands" (Polarsphere Books, 2021). He is the winner of the WeNaija Literary Contest (Non-Fiction, 2023). His works have appeared and are forthcoming at *Ake Review, Feral, Quills, Poemify, Melbourne-Culture, TNR, Nantygreen, Arting Arena* and elsewhere. He is the Editor-in-Chief of The Nigerian Review (TNR). He is a Senior Mentor at the Hill-Top Creative Arts Foundation and a Mentor of the SprinNG Writing Fellowship.

OKWUDILI NEBEOLISA is the author of Terminal Maladies (Autumn House Press 2024), winner of the 2023 Center for African American Poetry and Poetics Prize. He's a graduate of the Iowa Writers Workshop. His poems have appeared or are forthcoming in *Image, POETRY The Sewanee Review, The Southern Review,* and *The Threepenny Review.*

OMODERO DAVID OGHENEKARO is a writer from Delta State, Nigeria. He's currently an undergraduate student of Biomedical Technology at the University of Port Harcourt. His work has been published in *Lolwe, Strange Horizons, Fiyah Literary Magazine, The Dead lands, Yaba Left Review, Trampset* and elsewhere. He's a member of the Frontiers Collective.

OSAGIEDE BEST is an emerging Nigerian poet, essayist, playwright and storyteller. He reads philosophical and psychological literature in his free time; they greatly influence his writing and enlarge his thought horizon. He loves history, photography, physics, nature and biology. You can find his published article in Ajispeak, short story in Nnoko stories, his play of the absurdist tradition in African Writer Magazine, and his poems in *Afrihill* and *Kahalari Review.*

PATRICIA JABBEH WESLEY is a poet, fiction writer, a nonfiction writer, and an anti-war and human rights activist who began writing in her original home country of Liberia, West Africa, since the early age of thirteen. She immigrated to the United States with her family during the 14-year Liberian civil war, a war that has shaped her writing as a Diaspora African woman writer in the United States.has also had dozens of individual poems and memoir articles, and short stories anthologized and published in literary magazines, including *Harvard Review, Transition, Crab Orchard Review, Harvard Divinity Review, Prairie Schooner,* among others, and her work has been translated in Spanish, Italian, Finnish, and Hebrew.

PAMILERIN JACOB's poems have appeared in *POETRY*, *Lolwe*, *20.35 Africa*, *Agbowó*, *Frontier Poetry*, *The Rumpus* & elsewhere. He is the curator of Poetry Column-NND, a poetry column in Nigerian NewsDirect, a national newspaper.

RAHMA O. JIMOH is a winner of the Poetry Translation, Lagos-London competition '22 and a runner-up in the Abubakar Gimba short story prize '21. She is a participant in the Undertow Writing workshop and has been published or has works forthcoming in *Salt Hill Journal*, *Agbowo*, *Parentheses Art*, *Ake Review*, *Tinderbox Poetry*, *Olongo Africa*, *Lucent Dreaming*, *Isele Magazine*, *Tab Journal*, *Brittle Paper*, *Kalahari Review* & others. She is a lover of sunsets and monuments. She was a mentor in the 2023 SpringNg writing fellowship, she edits poetry at Olumo Review and is a prose reader at Chestnut Review.

RIDWAN BADAMASI writes from the ancient city of Kano in northern Nigeria. He is a Biochemistry undergrad in Bayero University. His works have appeared in Praxis Magazine, 20.35 Africa, Konya Shamsrumi, Salamander Ink Mag., and elsewhere. You can find him on X (Twitter): @RidhwanBadamasi.

S. SU'EDDIE VERSHIMA AGEMA is a multiple-award-winning writer, cultural activist, development consultant and one of Nigeria's most notable poets in 2022. He has won the Association of Nigerian Authors Poetry Prize (2014 & 2022), the Mandela Day Short Story Prize 2016 and was a finalist for the Nigeria Prize for Literature 2022. He is the author of *Bring Our Casket Home: Tales one shouldn't tell*. His other notable work is the poetry collection, *Memory and the Call of Waters*.

SALIMAH VALIANI is a poet, activist and researcher. Her poetry collection, 29 leads to love (Inanna 2021), was named the 2022 winner of the International Book Award for Contemporary Poetry. She has published four other poetry collections: breathing for breadth (TSAR 2005), Letter Out: Letter In (Inanna 2009) land of the sky (Inanna 2016) and Cradles (Daraja 2017). Her story-poem, Dear South

Africa, was selected for Praxis Magazine's 2019-2020 Online Chapbook Series. Valiani's audiobook, Love Pandemic, was released by Daraja Press (also in print) in 2022. Valiani lives in many places and crosses borders regularly. https://www.facebook.com/SalimahValianiPoet/.

SARPONG OSEI ASAMOAH is the author of the forthcoming chapbook "*YAANOM*" selected by Kwame Dawes and Chris Abani for the *African Poetry Book Fund.* He was a finalist for the *Bernardine Evaristo Prize for African Poetry 2023*, and is an alumni of Obsidian Foundation. His work has featured in *Lolwe, SAND Journal, Poetry Ireland Review, Protean Magazine, Agbowo Magazine, Olongo Africa Magazine* and elsewhere. He has worked at the *Library Of Africa and The African Diaspora, Tampered Press*, and is the creative director and host of *CanonPodcast; a podcast that speculates on Ghanaian poetics and poetry canon.*

SERVIO GBADAMOSI is a recipient of the 2016 *Ebedi International Writers Residency* fellowship where he co-wrote the chapbook, *A Half-Formed Thing*, with fellow residents, Ehi'zogie Iyeoman and Ikechukwu Nwaogu. His poetry collection, *A Tributary in Servitude* (WriteHouse Collective, 2015), won the 2015 *Association of Nigerian Authors Poetry Prize*, and was shortlisted runner-up for the 2018 *Wole Soyinka Prize for Literature in Africa*. His second poetry collection, *Where the Light Enters You* (Noirledge Publishing, 2021) was a finalist for the inaugural *Pan African Writers Association Poetry Prize*.

SODIQ ALABI is a writer and poet from Iwo, Nigeria. His poetry and other works have appeared in various journals including the Kalahari Review, Praxis, Sankofa and Arbiterz. His debut poetry collection, The Texture of Air was released in 2015 to critical acclaim. His second collection, Frozen Frames is forthcoming late 2023. Educated at the Universities of Ilorin and Sussex, Alabi works as a communications and engagement specialist. He lives in England with his wife and two daughters.

TADE IPADEOLA is a Nigerian poet, essayist, storyteller, translator, and lawyer. The recipient of many awards for both prose and poetry, he writes in both Yoruba and English. Among his main publications are three volumes of poetry – *A Time of Signs* (2000), *The Rain Fardel* (2005) and *The Sahara Testaments* (2013), the last of which won the Nigeria Prize for Literature; his latest collection is Cold Brew (2023). In 2009, his poem "Odidere" [Songbird] won the Delphic Laurel in poetry at the Delphic Games held in Jeju, South Korea. He has translated the novelist Daniel Fagunwa from the Yoruba, and W.H Auden, Tomas Tranströmer and Lu Xun into Yoruba.

TANURE OJAIDE has been the Frank Porter Graham Professor of Africana Studies since 2006. He is the author of more than twenty poetry collections which include *The Fate of Vultures*, *The Blood of Peace*, *The Tale of the Harmattan*, *Waiting for the Hatching of a Cockerel* (2008), *The Beauty I Have Seen*, *Songs of Myself: Quartet*, and *The Questioner: New Poems* (2018). His poems have been highly anthologized in dozens of major anthologies, including *The Poetry of Men's Lives: An International Anthology* (2004), *Emergency Kit: Poems for Strange Times* (1996), *Border Lines: Contemporary Poems in English* (1995), and *A World Assembly of Poets: Contemporary Poems* (2017).

TEMILOLUWA OKANMIYO OLUYEMI writes from the Western part of Nigeria. Most of her writings revolve around human experiences and the pains surrounding them all. She hopes to use this means of escape to open paths for others who are locked in their own pains.

TOLU OLORUNTOBA was born in Ibadan, Nigeria, where he also practiced medicine. He is the author of *The Junta of Happenstance* (Palimpsest Press / Anstruther Books), winner of the Canadian Griffin Poetry Prize and Governor General's Literary Award, and *Each One a Furnace* (McClelland & Stewart / Penguin Random House Canada), a Dorothy Livesay Poetry Prize finalist. His poetry has also appeared in Harvard Divinity Review, Columbia Journal,

Canadian Literature, and elsewhere. He was the 2022 League of Canadian Poets Anne Szumigalski Lecturer, and is a Civitella Ranieri fellow. He lives on Coast Salish lands in Surrey, western Canada.

TOPE LARAYETAN is a poet and writer. She is the 2023 winner of ODU's Graduate College Poetry Prize sponsored by the Academy of American Poets and the Poetry Society of Virginia. Her works have appeared or are forthcoming in Poets.org, Agbowo, The Shallow Tales Review, and the maiden edition of the International Sisi Eko anthology.

UCHECHUKWU PETER UMEZURIKE is an assistant professor in the Department of English, University of Calgary, Canada. His teaching and research interests include African and African Diaspora literatures, postcolonial literatures, gender and sexuality, cultural studies, and creative writing. An award-winning creative writer, Umezurike is the author of literary works such as *there's more* (2023), *Double Wahala, Double Trouble* (2021), *Wish Maker* (2021), and a co-editor of *Wreaths for a Wayfarer* (2020).

ZAMA MADINANA is a South African poet based in Johannesburg. His work has appeared in *The Shallow Tales Review*, *Stanzas*, *Africanwriter*, *Poetry Potion* and other literary publications. His poems have been published in Zimbabwe, Nigeria, and the USA. Madinana's work focuses on love, politics and social issues. In 2021, he won the third prize in the *Sol Plaatje EU Poetry Award*. His poetry chapbook, *Water & Lights*, was published in June 2021. He has performed his poetry in various locations, including Cape Town, Mozambique, and Botswana.

ZADA HANMER is a writer living and working in Johannesburg. She is currently studying an Honours degree in Creative Writing.

EDITORS

JIDE SALAWU is a literary scholar and Nigerian poet. He is the current managing editor of *OlongoAfrica* and founding conversationalist at Brown Bamboo. Salawu's work has appeared in *Literary Review of Canada*, *Prairie Schooner*, *Rattle*, *Transition*, *Grain*, *This Magazine*, *Lolwe*, *Poetry Society of America*, *Fiddlehead*, *This Magazine*, *LitHub*, *Popula*, *The Mantle*, *The Republic*, *Preachy*, *CBC*, and *Public Parking*. He is the author of *Preface for Leaving Homeland* published under African Poetry Book Fund, and *Contraband Bodies* forthcoming in Fall 2025 under NeWest Press (Canada) and Narrative Landscape (Nigeria). A pushcart nominee, Salawu was shortlisted for Babishai Niwe African Poetry Prize in 2015 and 2017. He won the James Patrick Folinsbee award for creative writing at the English and Film Studies (EFS) program, University of Alberta. In 2022, he won the Vancouver Manuscript Intensive Fellowship. His research work has appeared in*Africology*,*Journal of African Cultural Studies*,*African Identities*, and forthcoming in *Journal of African Literature Association*. Currently, he is rounding off his PhD program at the EFS program of the University of Alberta, Canada.

RASAQ MALIK GBOLAHAN is a graduate of the University of Ibadan. He is a co-founder of Àtẹ́lẹwọ́, a journal devoted to publishing literary work written in the Yorùbá language. He is the author of two poetry chapbooks, *No Home In This Land* and *The Other Names Of Grief*. His work has appeared or is forthcoming in *African American Review*, *Antigonish Review*, *Colorado Review*, *Crab Orchard Review*, *Lit Hub*, *Michigan Quarterly Review*, *Minnesota Review*, *New Orleans Review*, *Prairie Schooner*, *Poet Lore*, *Poetry Northwest*, *Rattle*, *Salt Hill*, *Spillway*, *Southern Humanities Review*, *Stand*, *Transition*, *Verse Daily*, and elsewhere. He won Honorable Mention in 2015 Best of the Net for his poem "Elegy", published in One. In 2017, Rattle and Poet Lore nominated his poems for the Pushcart Prize. He was shortlisted for Brunel International African Poetry Prize in 2017. He was a finalist for Sillerman First Book for African Poets in 2018. Gbolahan is currently a PhD Candidate at the English program of the University of Nebraska-Lincoln, United States.